CHAIN REACTIONS

Other books by John Weisenberger

What is Global Marketing For Small Business?
ISBN: 978-1479236893
http://www.amazon.com/dp/B0095M3QYG

CHAIN REACTIONS

*How to Create Massive Customer Loyalty and Profits
Using Customer Experience Management*

(Second Edition)

John Weisenberger

Copyright © 2014, 2015 Arcadium Group LLC

All rights reserved.

ISBN-10: 1499758855
ISBN-13: 978-1499758856

"Chain Reactions: How to Create Massive Customer Loyalty and Profits Using Customer Experience Management" is provided as information only. At the time it was compiled it was believed to be accurate and up to date. The author and publisher assumes no liability for any errors, or for any actions caused by following the information in this publication. We encourage everyone entering into a new business or a new phase of business to work closely with an accountant and a lawyer to insure that they are operating in accordance with all laws and regulations.

A word about Links: websites accessed by hypertext appearing in this publication may be independent from, and may have been developed by parties other than the author/publisher. As such the author/publisher cannot and does not warrant the accuracy of information contained in such websites. The listing of an organization in this publication should not be construed as an endorsement of its services or products. Visiting any other site is at your sole risk and the author/publisher will not be responsible or liable for any damages in connection with linking to any other site.

Affiliate Disclaimer: From time to time, the author/publisher may promote, endorse, or suggest products and/or services for sale that are not their own. This may be based on a review of that product, the author/publisher's personal or professional relationship with that person or company, and/or a previous positive experience with the person or company who's product the author/publisher recommends. In many cases, the author/publisher will be compensated via a commission if you decide to purchase that product based on their recommendation.

DCMA Disclaimer: Every attempt has been made by the author/publisher to provide acknowledgement of the sources used for the material in this book. If you believe that your work has been copied in a way that constitutes copyright infringement, please follow the Notice and Procedures for Making Claims of Copyright Infringement available at the publisher's website.

Published by:
Arcadium Group LLC
P.O. Box 2681
Stow, OH 44224
www.Arcadium-Group.com

CONTENTS

	Preface	7
	Introduction	11
Chapter 1	Creating Powerful Reactions	17
Chapter 2	The Voice of the Customer	43
Chapter 3	Your Role as a Reaction Creator	67
Chapter 4	Reaction ROI	99
Chapter 5	Chain Reactions Marketing	111
Chapter 6	How to Get Started	115
	Conclusion	117
	Case Studies	121
	Resources	131
	About The Author	145

CHAIN REACTIONS

"A smile can cause a chain reaction of happiness"

-Eduardo Monroy

PREFACE

Admittedly I'm a bit picky when it comes to customer service standards. After 30-plus years of traveling around the world on behalf of my Fortune 500 employers I've experienced just about every aspect of the hospitality industry. I've also been on both sides of the negotiating table having been a customer, strategic alliance partner, or as a global supplier to other businesses.

During my travels I've experienced best-in-class customer service at hotels, on airlines, on trains, in taxis, restaurants and bars. I've also had some horrendous experiences too.

In my business travels I've experienced strategic alliance partners, customers and suppliers who know how to make a positive first impression on a visiting executive. I've also encountered businesses who I immediately removed from consideration the moment I walked through their front door.

It's regrettable because many of the bad experiences I've encountered could have been easily prevented if only the business owners and their employees had been aware of the emotional reactions they were creating in their prospects and customers.

For example, I'll never forget the exceptional experience I had the first time I stayed at the Royal Park Hotel in Tokyo.

From the very first moment I stepped out of the airport taxi, I was greeted with a warm a welcoming reception that extended all the way through check-in until my baggage was delivered to my room by a smiling young man who expected no gratuity for his service.

Now contrast this with my recent experience at a similarly priced hotel in the U.K. where I had to stand and wait at the reception desk while a frowning desk clerk talked on the phone without even acknowledging my presence.

CHAIN REACTIONS

To make matters worse, after what seemed like an inordinate amount of time, the unsmiling desk clerk finally asked for my name and then began to multi-task; looking up my reservation and asking for my credit card while continuing her conversation on the telephone.

It was only after seeing that another guest had come in behind me that she finally ended her telephone conversation and then hastily slid a room key and signature paper in front of me; quickly mentioned the operating hours of the restaurant, and then pointed me to the lifts with barely another word said.

By the end of my stay several other negative aspects of my experience at this particular hotel clearly demonstrated to me the noticeable differences in each hotel's desire to provide their guests with a pleasant and memorable 5-Star customer experience. Differences I won't belabor, but suffice it to say, I will not be going back to that U.K. hotel ever again.

Now, you may be wondering why I told you this particular story?

I told you this story because stories are how we humans remember and communicate our experiences. It's the stories in our heads that create the positive or negative emotions we attach to a particular customer experience; so creating more positive and memorable stories in our customers' heads is an area I'll go into deeper later in the book.

I also used this comparison of my hotel check-in experiences because I think most people can relate to the typical check-in process and all the possible emotional reactions that could occur in a customer during the process. Emotional reactions that can be either positive or negative depending on how we perceive we're being treated.

It's the emotional reactions we have during each of these "links in the check-in chain" that ultimately determine how we remember the check-in process and whether we decide the experience was excellent or poor.

And the check-in process is only just the beginning of an even longer *Customer Journey* chain of events that encompasses all the other

Touch Points and *Moments of Truth* a customer will encounter during a stay at any hotel.

In fact, every customer experience story has a beginning, a middle and an ending; with the ending actually being the most important part of the story; which I'll explain a bit later.

Which brings me to the point of this book.

Creating life-long, loyal, customers that will deliver a continuous stream of revenue and profits for your business, year after year, is really all about making sure that each link in the customer experience "chain of emotional reactions" is positioning you and your business as the best and only logical solution to whatever it is your customer, client or patient wants.

In fact, when you develop truly loyal customers, you won't need to be finding new prospects each and every year. Consistently deliver exceptional customer experiences and your existing customers will send you all the new referrals you can handle which will save you the need for expensive advertising or discounted price promotions. And what could be better than that?

So with all that said, if you take away just one thing from reading this book, I'd like you to remember this. **All businesses really sell just one thing: Reactions!**

The reactions you create are your actual product. And as soon as you begin to see your business as a reaction-creating machine, you'll begin to think about your business and its operations differently.

In *Chain Reactions*, I'll show you how to think differently about the reactions you create and how to put Customer Experience Marketing to work in your own business to create the massive customer loyalty and profits you so richly deserve.

CHAIN REACTIONS

INTRODUCTION

Like dominos falling one after the other, Chain Reactions occur in the business world every day. Most people just don't recognize them or think about them. But they are there. And they are powerful as you will see.

I wrote this book for you, the small and medium sized business owner, because I believe that differentiation based on Customer Experience will be the key to all future business success moving forward.

I also wrote it because I know that customer satisfaction and loyalty can be (and should be) managed using a system of proven marketing strategies and tactics that will create a multi-linked chain of loyalty building, profit generating, reactions in your customers, clients or patients, that can ultimately power your business for life.

That's why I've put everything I've learned over the past 30 years (working for and with some of the world's best companies such as United Parcel Service, Rockwell Automation and Honeywell International) into a Customer Experience Marketing training program I call the Chain Reactions Marketing System.™ A training program that I hope to earn the right to introduce to you at the end of this book.

Why focus on the Customer Experience? Big companies like Apple, Amazon, Zappos and many others are all creating thousands and millions of loyal, fanatic customers using Customer Experience Marketing as a key business strategy. I believe small businesses should be doing it too.

Sadly, however, there are still far too many small and medium sized businesses around the world that could be, and should be, differentiating themselves by providing their customers with an overall emotional experience that's superior to anything being provided by their competitors. But they're not.

And that's why I wrote this book.

CHAIN REACTIONS

I wrote it to help you understand that the way you brand yourself with your marketing, your pricing, your employee dress code, website content, logo or retail shop curb appeal; everything you do should be about creating emotional chain reactions that create powerful customer experiences because the businesses that create the best reactions will always make the most money!

I also wrote it because I believe that (if you're like I was when I first started out) many small business owners and managers have some misconceptions about what Customer Experience Marketing is and isn't.

For example, you may think that:

1. Customer Experience Marketing is only important for consumer oriented B2C businesses.

    This is not true. B2B customers today expect the same customer service levels and experiences they've become accustomed to in their personal lives.

2. You may have the misconception that Customer Experience Marketing (CEM) is the same thing as Customer Relationship Management (CRM)

    Again not true. CRM is about using technology to organize, automate and synchronize sales, marketing, customer service and technical support. CEM is about people and the emotions that they experience when doing business with you.

3. You may have the misconception that your number one Customer Experience objective should be winning more new customers.

    Actually, yes and no. Your number one goal should be to create more loyal customers who buy from you over and over again plus refer you to all their friends and relatives; thus winning you more new customers too.

4. You may have the misconception that you need to have expensive software tools like Salesforce.com or Oracle to implement Customer Experience Marketing.

    Also not true. I'll show you several practical alternatives to large and expensive software systems and tools.

5. And lastly, you may have the misconception that you need a huge budget and a large staff to deliver exceptional customer experiences.

    Also not true. Most customer experience improvements can be implemented with little or no incremental costs. For example, how much does it cost to always remember to smile at your customers and call them by their first name?

After hearing so many small business owners recite the same misconceptions and seeing so many small businesses go through the very same brand differentiation struggles, I knew I had to share my lessons learned with the world.

So with that as my goal, in this book I'll present four central ideas:

1. First, I want you to understand that you really can grow your business, significantly, using a Customer Experience Marketing strategy and tactics that won't cost a you a lot of time and money to implement. Others are doing it and you can too!

2. Second, the very best way to attract and retain more loyal and profitable customers is by providing them a Customer Experience that is differentiated and superior to your competitors'. There's no one else in business exactly like you so make sure your customers come to realize that fact so they choose you over anyone else.

3. Third, your customer's perception of your business, and the emotional reactions they feel when doing business

with you, is reality.

It doesn't matter how well you think you're doing, it only matters how well your customers <u>feel</u> you're doing.

You absolutely must be collecting and analyzing Voice of the Customer (VOC) feedback so you can objectively measure where you need to improve your business in order to provide an exceptional and differentiated customer experience. Without actual VOC feedback as a reality check, your version of reality may be very distorted compared to how your customers actually feel.

4. Fourth, you need to understand that you can't do everything yourself and still deliver an exceptional Customer Experience.

You'll need to learn to delegate all the time-wasting, non-income generating, tasks you do every day to others so you can focus on doing those "highest and best use" things that only you can do to deliver an exceptional customer experience. I'll show you how to do that too.

So who can benefit by reading this book?

Customer Experience Marketing can be used by anyone. Small business owners, solopreneurs, marketing managers, sales managers or anyone else who wants to grow their business in today's overly crowded and commoditized marketplace where customers now have all the power.

This book can be used by:

- **Automotive related businesses:** Dealers, Towing, Glass, Painting, Body Shops, Tire Shops, Transmission and other auto service businesses.
- **Health Care related businesses:** Dentist, Dermatologist, Elder Care, Hospitals, OBGYN, Ophthalmologist,

Pediatricians, Plastic Surgeons, Primary Care, Psychiatrists

- **Home related businesses:** Carpet Cleaning, Electrical, Handymen, Heating & A/C, Housecleaning, Painting, Plumbing, Remodeling, Roofing, Windows
- **Outdoor related businesses**: Bicycles, Fencing, Landscaping, Irrigation, Lawn Mower repair, Lawn Treatment, Lawn and Yard work, Mulch and Topsoil, Pool & Spa Services, Tree Services
- **Professional Service businesses:** Lawyers, CPAs, Financial Planners, Engineers, Designers
- **Retailers, Manufactures**, and many more.

Regardless of your type of industry or profession, Chain Reactions will show you how to create massive customer loyalty and profits by managing the entire Customer Experience from beginning to end. All you have to do is take the necessary action to implement what you'll learn.

So with that all said, if you're ready to learn how to create Customer Experience Chain Reactions that will totally transform your business results, let's get started!

John Weisenberger
Stow, Ohio USA
June, 2014

CHAIN REACTIONS

CHAPTER 1

Creating Powerful Reactions

A positive attitude causes a chain reaction
of positive thoughts, events and outcomes.
It is a catalyst and it sparks
extraordinary results.

-Wade Boggs

Have you ever experienced any of these challenges?

1. A longtime customer or client, who you've done business with for years, suddenly stops doing business with you for no apparent reason?

2. A competitor moves in across town and "buys" several of your existing customers by advertising introductory new client pricing 25% lower than yours?

3. A visitor to your restaurant, hotel or health care clinic doesn't complain to you directly, but then tells everyone on Yelp, TripAdvisor, Angie's List, or some other industry review website, that they'll never do business with you again.

Well it's happened to me and I've seen these types of things happen to other businesses too.

Over the years I've seen a lot of businesses, big and small, handle these types of customer loyalty challenges with various degrees of success; all depending on how aware they were about what their customers were feeling and saying about their brands on social media and in the marketplace.

CHAIN REACTIONS

How successful any business is at handling these types of challenges really all depends on whether or not they are willing to accept that we are now living in a new "Age of the Customer" where both B2C and B2B customers now have virtually unlimited choices and power in deciding where and how they choose to spend their money.

Businesses that understand that the customer now has all the power, and are willing to work hard at delivering exceptional Customer Experiences that create long-term customer loyalty, those are the businesses that can survive these types of challenges successfully and come out the other side with even higher loyalty and retention rates.

On the other hand, those businesses that fail to see or acknowledge this shift in power will ultimately lose their longtime customers resulting in a steady declined in their revenues and profits. And that's unfortunate because it doesn't have to be that way.

The good news is, each and every one of the customer loyalty challenges described earlier can be overcome if you're willing to acknowledge that it's a totally new world today and that how the customer actually feels about your business is the real key to all future business success.

Make Customer Experience Marketing the cornerstone of your marketing strategy and you'll drive positive business change, deliver superior Return on Investment (ROI) and create a competitive advantage for your business.

Ignore the customer experience and you'll quickly find new customers in short supply and your long time customers defecting over to your competitor's products and services.

But that won't happen to you because I'm going to teach you how to create a differentiated customer experience that will set your brand and business apart from all the others in your market or industry.

But before I do that, please indulge me while I tell you another story.

In July of 2013 I went to the U.K. to evaluate a company as a potential strategic alliance partner for a new product I was developing.

I had selected this particular company based on the positive first impression I had after reviewing the company's Website and product literature, and after having spoken with the Managing Director of the company on the phone several times.

Now on the surface this company seemed to be a great candidate for an alliance. The Managing Director seemed to know the market and we both seemed to have similar business and partnering philosophies.

So in the first link of my customer experience chain of reactions this company had passed the "discovery link" with a strong enough first impression to warrant my associate Ashwini (a.k.a. Ash) and I making a trip to the U.K. for an in-person meeting at the company's headquarters.

In fact, upon first meeting the Managing Director of the company (a very professional looking English gentleman who picked us up at our hotel wearing a three-piece suit and driving a very expensive car) everything seemed to be moving in the right direction as Ash and I entered the second, "evaluation link" of the customer experience chain.

It was only upon our arrival at the company's headquarters that our perception of the company drastically changed and here's why.

After driving for about an hour we finally arrived at the company's headquarters located in a 200+ year-old house in the small English town of Sandbach whereupon the Managing Director parked the car in a very small side alley next to an overflowing trash dumpster.

We then entered the headquarters house - who's windows and doors were flaking paint and in need of substantial repair - through a small back door and proceeded up a narrow flight of creaking stairs to the Managing Director's second floor "master bedroom office" whereupon he immediately opened a small window to allow some

CHAIN REACTIONS

fresh air into his non-air-conditioned office.

He then pulled out a pipe, lit it up, and then swiveled the computer monitor on his desk towards us to begin a presentation on the capabilities of his products and company.

Now somewhere between parking the car next to the dumpster and beginning the presentation in the smoke filled master bedroom office, Ash and I had both already made up our minds that this was not a company we wanted to do business with.

Even if the company's technology and products had been very good, the emotional reaction both Ash and I had to what we were seeing and experiencing was so strong we both immediately knew there was no way we were going to risk partnering with this company.

Consequently, we both politely listened to the Managing Director's presentation; asked our questions; spoke with the company's head of Engineering; had a pleasant lunch with them in an even older English tavern; and then went back to the hotel where we crossed the company off our list of potential alliance partners.

Now you're probably wondering why I told you this particular story?

I told it to illustrate my point that attracting, winning and then keeping a customer requires a multi-link chain of customer experiences that must create a positive customer reaction during each and every step of the customer journey chain. Perform poorly on any one of the links in the chain of reactions and you'll lose the sale.

Even worse, slack off on any of the links in the chain and you could lose an existing customer. And statistics show it will cost you six to ten time more to replace that lost customer than it would have been to keep them[1]

So why else did I tell you this story the way I remember it?

I also told you this story because, as I mentioned earlier, stories are how we remember the emotional reactions we have to an experience.

Our emotions actually determine the things we remember and the mind uses stories to make sense of the emotional reactions we feel. Consequently, as soon as we experience something, we quickly fit that experience into a story in our heads. What we keep from our experiences and our reactions to these experiences (positive or negative) is our memory stored in the form of a story.

So when it comes to customer perception versus reality, when a customer recounts an experience to a friend on social media or on a review website, they're actually sharing the perceived story of the experience they created in their heads, not the actual experience. That's why it's so important to always remember that the customer's perception (right or wrong) is reality as far as they're concerned.

Consequently, when a customer makes a decision to buy from a business, or to remain a loyal customer, they're choosing between the stories of their perceived experiences. The actual experience itself has no real relevance in their choice.

So how are the customer experience stories we remember created?

Most of the individual moments of a customer experience are lost and don't make it into the story customers remember in their heads except for significant moments and the ending of the experience.

For example, Dr. Daniel Kahneman, one of the founders of behavioral economics[2] and winner of the 2002 Nobel Prize in Economic Sciences, studied the pain experienced by patients during colonoscopies – you see in the past colonoscopies used to be very painful procedures; today they put you under and you just wake up after it's over – and discovered it was how the procedure ended that determined what the patient actually remembered of the experience.

In his studies that monitored how much pain the patients said they were feeling during the procedure, versus how much they remembered feeling after the procedure, the patients who said they had more pain remembered it as a less painful experience if the procedure ended on a less painful note.

Essentially, Dr. Kahneman discovered that doctors were able to make patients remember a better experience by prolonging the procedure a little bit longer so it ended on a less painful note. Which brings me to my next point.

Every experience during a customer's engagement with your business, like every story ever written, has a beginning, a middle and an ending.

And although the ending is the most important part of the story, having a clearly scripted Customer Journey Map (which we'll talk about a bit later) with a well thought out beginning, middle and ending is an essential part of delivering the emotional Chain Reactions required to make the stories about your brand and your business the most compelling and positive stories being told in the marketplace.

Because after all, your brand reputation is nothing more than the stories people tell about you when you're not in the room.

So what are some of the keys to creating exceptionally powerful customer experience stories for your brand?

Here are several tips you can use:

1. **Walk a mile in your customer's shoes.** Look at your business through your customer's eyes and ask yourself: What type of experience would I want?

    Then map out your *Customer Journey* process: When do customers first interact with your company? How do they evaluate your offers? How do they make their purchase and use your product or service? When do they stop using what you offer?

    Creating memorable stories about your brand is also about more than simply avoiding any negative customer experiences. It's about creating truly memorable experiences that will leave your customers wanting more and willing to tell your story to their friends and family.

One way to do that if your service has any type of pain or bad news associated with it (such as a car in need of a major service repair) is by extending the length of your customer's experience or giving them something unexpected so it ends on an extremely positive note. Doing this will provide a greater opportunity to create a positive experience and build a stronger relationship.

2. **Don't fight the VoC (Voice of the Customer)** There's no better way to determine what's working and what's not than gathering VoC feedback from the customers themselves.

Use review sites like Yelp, TripAdvisor, Healthgrades or Angie's List to see what your customers are saying about your business and then determine the best way to improve their experience.

Also, be sure to respond to your customers' feedback on these review sites to ensure their opinions are valued.

And lastly, don't neglect responding to any negative reviews. Negative reviews provide a valuable opportunity to address, salvage and potentially build a loyal (and more profitable) customer relationship.

3. **Become their Trusted Advisor.** Instead of focusing on selling just your product or service, offer expert advice on whatever is the best solution for your customer's problem -- even if it's outside of your current offering. This type of concern for the customer's total wellbeing will build trust with your customers and helps you establish long-lasting relationships.

4. **Improve the "necessary evils" parts of the process.** Many small business owners and entrepreneurs focus

primarily on creating and delivering their product or service because it's what they enjoy doing. And that's not surprising because we all know there are many "necessary evils" in any business that are not always fun.

However, it's these necessary evils that typically require the most disciplined attention to detail because they are often the most significant factor in delivering a great customer experience.

For example, which areas or business processes do you frequently try to avoid? What's the payment, billing or product return experience like? What's the product support experience like? What happens immediately after you finish delivering your service?

Consider making small adjustments to improve the areas of your business you commonly dread so you can deliver a complete "end to end" customer experience superior to any your local (or global) competitors can supply.

Your customers will appreciate the added attention or ease of doing business factor, and move you towards that trusted partner status mentioned earlier rather than considering you just another one-time transactional supplier.

5. **Don't Rush.** Moving too fast is another common mistake many small businesses make. Now that's not to say that getting the job done as quickly and as efficiently as possible is not a priority. However, spending a few extra minutes to make sure your customer is fully satisfied will be worth it in the long run because people want to feel special.

Take just the right amount of time and showing your customers just a little extra attention will result in a superior experience that can create more positive word of mouth recommendations and increased referrals for your business overall.

Just be aware that the opposite is also true: If your customers feel rushed, or that they haven't received any real special attention, they're likely to leave with a negative experience and probably won't come back.

At the end of the day you may not have an exact match for your competitors' offering but you do have complete control over your customers' experience; and ultimately the story they tell themselves and others about their experience. Take the time to provide an unforgettably great customer experience and it will pay off more than you can imagine.

So, with the preceding tips in mind, let's talk a little bit more about why brand differentiation based on Customer Experience is so important in today's economy.

Standing Out From The Crowd

Whether you're selling a product, a service, a project or a process, I firmly believe that customer experience is the only true brand differentiator available to small businesses today.

In today's new "Age of the Customer", most products and services have become commodities available from multiple suppliers and distribution channels around the world.

So the big question becomes, how do you make your business stand out from all the others in the market?

Some experts would tell you that you need to maintain brand differentiation through technical or process innovation, but I would say that, for most small businesses, differentiation based on a true product or service innovation just isn't sustainable over time; because, let's face it, most innovations can be (and will be) copied and commoditized eventually.

But here's the good news: The one thing that truly can't be copied is you!

Your personality, your skills, your perspective on things and the personal relationships you and your employees have with your customers. How well you solve your customer's problems and how you make them feel when they do business with you, that's something that can't be commoditized!

So regardless of what you've read or heard from others about new product innovation being the key to competitive advantage, the reality is, trying to come up with a new product or service innovation every year or two typically just isn't practical in for most small businesses in today's hyper competitive global, or even local, economy.

So let's rule out product or technical innovation as our marketing strategy for brand differentiation.

Now let's talk about using low price as a brand differentiator.

A second marketing strategy many businesses try to use to differentiate themselves is to be the low cost provider in their market or industry.

I strongly oppose this strategy because anyone who's tried it knows it's a margin killing race to the bottom that ruins profitability and assures that no one actually wins the competition in the long run.

To me it's unfortunate that anyone still believes cutting price is the best way to win new business.

In fact, several marketing studies have shown that roughly 86% of consumers are actually willing to pay more for a better, more satisfying, customer experience.

Let me say that again: 86% of consumers are actually willing to pay more for a better, more satisfying, customer experience!

Statistics also show that public companies that differentiate on Customer Experience consistently outpace their competitors in revenue growth and in overall shareholder value created.

So the bottom line is, differentiating your business based on providing the best possible overall buying, delivery and customer support experience is just good business. And the one marketing strategy that is clearly doable by any business who has the vision and determination to do so is Customer Experience Marketing.

> 91% of unhappy customers will not **willingly** do business with you again. However, resolve a complaint in the customer's favor and they will do business with you again 70% of the time.
>
> *Source: Lee Resources*

CHAIN REACTIONS

Creating Loyal Customers

Let me ask you this: is it better to have satisfied customers or loyal customers?

The answer is, loyal customers are better.

A loyal customer is a customer who resists switching to another brand, or to doing business with another company, whereas a satisfied customer may or may not be loyal.

So the ultimate goal of any Customer Experience Marketing program is to create and retain more loyal customers who will stick with your business and provide a continuous life time of profits.

In addition to their loyalty, the second behavior you want from your customers is Advocacy.

Advocacy is a behavior that goes beyond loyalty.

An advocate is as customer who tells their friends, their family, or their colleagues about how much they enjoy doing business with you and your company.

Customer advocacy is so important in today's social media age, it has become a key component of most company's metrics and Key Performance Indicators (KPI).

That's because it's been shown that customer recommendations have a significant influence on the acquisition of new customers to the point that even just one positive or negative mention of a brand on a social media channel is shown to have a huge effect on a businesses' overall financial performance.

Effectively, the more your brand delivers positive customer experiences, the greater the amount of social media and word of mouth advocacy that can be created which is likely to drive even more new customers to your business.

It's also been shown that loyal customers who advocate for your business also tend to be customers that purchase more products, more often. Often referred to as gaining a greater share of the customer's wallet.

And because expanding sales through acquiring a greater share of wallet from existing customers cost 6-10 times less than acquiring a new customer, improving customer loyalty by providing outstanding Customer Experiences is clearly one of the best and most profitable approaches to increasing your businesses' long term revenues and profits.

Emotional Reactions Build Loyalty

One of the ultimate goals of any business is to find an answer to the age old question, "How do we get a customer to choose us, and only us, forever?"

The answer to that question is, you need to create an emotional attachment that makes it hard for them to leave.

When a customer develops loyalty to a product or service, he or she develops a deep-rooted emotional commitment, along with psychological reasoning that spurs the person to return for more.

Loyal customers have an emotional connection to a brand because the value they believe they receive goes beyond a pure monetary transaction.

It's just human nature to feel some kind of loyalty toward something that you feel an emotional connection to. That includes brands.

In fact, surveys have shown the typical buying decision process for most customers is more emotional than rational with estimates in most product and service categories indicating a 70% emotional to 30% rational buying decision ratio.

So the question becomes, how can your business create the emotional reactions and connections that will create long-term customer loyalty?

Here are the three primary factors that must be present at all times in order to create long-term customer loyalty.

1. **Stability:** Customers become emotionally involved with a brand when it sends a <u>consistent brand message</u> they can identify with.

2. **Sustainability:** Customers become emotionally involved with a brand when they expect that brand to be available to them for a long period of time, or for a specific period of time with a predetermined and accepted end date.

3. **Security:** Customers become emotionally involved with a brand when that brand gives them a feeling of peace-of-mind. In other words, when they feel they can trust a brand.

Businesses that keep these three emotional factors in mind as they develop their brand's products and marketing strategies will naturally achieve better customer loyalty results.

That's because people naturally want to feel stability, sustainability, and security in their lives and those desires don't stop when it comes to choosing products and services.

So, what are some of the big brands doing to make sure they emotionally connect with their customers?

Let's start with Apple who has achieved a level of brand loyalty which most manufacturers can only dream of. After all if the majority of your customers won't even consider looking at your competitors' products before buying your latest model, how can you lose?

In fact, according to 2014 figures from Asymco, Apple has taken 62% of the smartphone industry's $216B net operating profits over the last six years. As a measure of this dominance Samsung was second with 26%.

So how does Apple achieve this customer loyalty dominance?

Among several of the marketing strategies Apple uses to wow customers, one of the areas Apple excels in is the consistency/stability factor mentioned earlier.

For example, all of Apple's software products have the same basic look and feel. Because of this consistency, customers who already own

Apple products have a good idea of what they'll be getting before they make a purchase. They know that it will be easy to adapt to new hardware and this makes them more open to making a repeat purchase.

Harley-Davidson

Another brand known for its extremely loyal customers is Harley-Davidson. Even for those who aren't motorcycle enthusiasts, the name Harley-Davidson brings to mind the qualities that the brand embodies: Freedom, pride, independence, and rugged individualism.

By consistently cultivating and reinforcing these emotional feelings in every interaction with its customers, Harley-Davidson has become the #1 motorcycle brand in the United States.

How does the Harley brand do it? What Harley-Davidson has done so well is to show consumers that buying a Harley is actually buying into a lifestyle and a community. Yes, the quality of the motorcycles it manufactures is important, but the community it supports and fosters is what fosters an emotional tie to its fans.

Whole Foods

Whole Foods has rapidly risen from a local natural foods market in Austin, Texas, to a global health-food powerhouse because of its loyal following of health conscious consumers. Founded on the principle that natural foods and farming practices are integral to leading a healthy and conscientious life, Whole Foods has become the go-to for consumers who want to align with these values.

> According to Scott Matthews at CrowdTwist.com, *"Whole Foods, like most successful brands, uses a multi-faceted approach to building and consistently reinforcing its bond with customers. It is constantly experimenting with innovative technology, including placing sustainable greenhouses on top of its stores to providing the freshest produce to customers.*
>
> *The brand also find ways to evangelize about the importance of its mission directly to consumers through its outstanding customer service and loyalty efforts, or more widely via blogs, magazines, in-store promotions, and social*

media to create an environment that inspires a healthy lifestyle.

It's this kind of passionate and innovating thinking that shows shoppers that Whole Foods is tireless in its pursuit of improving the state of health and food production around the world.

When people buy from Whole Foods, they know they are supporting a change in themselves and the world they want to live in, and that kind of emotional bond is difficult to break."

So the bottom line is, when it comes to creating emotional reactions that build customer loyalty, there is no standard playbook or roadmap. Loyalty is inherently personal and particular to each individual because it's based on the emotions I covered earlier. Apple, Harley-Davidson, Whole Foods, and many other brands, all understand this and have built their businesses on it.

It's no longer enough to provide the best product or service. What will always remain are the emotional bonds brands build by engaging with customers on a personalized level and fostering genuine emotional connections at every turn. Remember that truly great brands aim for customers' hearts; not their wallets!

The Red Napkin Treatment

As we just covered, a big part of creating loyalty building customer experiences is to deliver personalized and unexpected surprises that foster emotional connections.

One way to do that is through the use of a clever "Red Napkin Treatment" used in the bar and restaurant industry that can also be applied in many other industries where first time customers, clients or patients are waiting for service. For example, automotive service departments.

The Red Napkin Treatment works like this:

Any employee who greats or checks-in customers should ask the customer if this is their first visit to your business. This check-in person could be the hostess at a restaurant or an auto service associate who checks in a customer's car at the service garage.

If the customer's answer is yes, you "tag them" with some sort of colored item (red, blue, green, your choice) that identifies them as a first time customer.

This colored item could be an actual red cocktail napkin that's placed under water glasses on a customer's table if your business is a restaurant or bar, or for an auto dealer service department, tire center, etc., it could simply be by giving the customer a specially labeled bottle of water or some other type of item that can be used to identify the individual as a new service customer.

The basic idea of the "Red Napkin Treatment" is to identify new customers so they can be treated with extra attention in order to make an exceptional first impression.

Which leads us to the next step in the process.

After the new customer has been identified, the restaurant manager,

CHAIN REACTIONS

service department manager, etc., can walk around the restaurant or service department waiting room and approach any new customers to welcome them or ask them how the service was after the meal, oil change, etc..

For example, the manager at a restaurant could offer to provide the new customer with a complimentary desert or the automotive service manager could offer a coupon for a free tire rotation with their next oil change. Whatever is best to make that new customer feel special.

Now as a slight twist on the Red Napkin Treatment, let me tell you another story about a recent experience I had with a local landscaping company and how the owner of that landscaping company collected feedback from me while also making a great first impression.

Earlier this year I ordered some landscaping mulch for the tree islands in our yard. I had chosen a particular landscaping company (Turf Trimmers Landscaping Inc.) because I remembered my wife saying she had spoken with them a few weeks earlier at a local business showcase event - held every year at our local high school – and that they seemed "nice."

So knowing nothing more about Turf Trimmers than what my wife told me, I decided to call them to purchase what I believe is a true commodity product -- mulch is, after all, just ground up wood and dirt -- like I had purchased from several other landscaping companies over the years.

Anyway, I telephoned Turf Trimmers where a very pleasant and professional woman reviewed the various types and colors of mulch Turf Trimmers carried, asked me when, where and how I wanted the order delivered, and then took my credit card information over the phone. Not that much different from the experiences I've had with all of the other landscaping companies I have dealt with in the past.

But here's what happened next.

The delivery truck driver arrives at my door the following Saturday morning and politely confirms the order and where I wanted to have the rather large pile of mulch placed in my driveway. The one thing that was different is that he apologetically informed me that he had forgotten my order receipt and that he would have it mailed to me. I said no big deal and accepted the delivery.

About an hour later there was another knock at my door whereupon the owner of Turf Trimmers presented me with a pink copy of my order receipt while apologizing for not having it available from the driver.

We then chatted a bit longer while he asked me several questions about the driver and my satisfaction with the delivery service, the quality of the mulch, everything you would expect from someone collecting customer satisfaction feedback on the experience of buying and taking delivery of an order of mulch.

It was only after the owner left that I began reflecting on our conversation and I began to wonder if I had just experienced the Red Napkin Treatment myself?

Was the missing pink receipt the equivalent of a red napkin where I had been identified on the phone order as a new customer and the owner used the excuse of delivering the missing receipt as a reason for contacting me in person?

I may never know.

What I do know, however, is that if the personalized visit was a pre-planned, orchestrated, way of collecting customer feedback then my hats off to Turf Trimmers for being on top of their Customer Experience Marketing game.

On the other hand, if the missing receipt delivery wasn't a conscious marketing strategy to create a personalized customer connection and to demonstrate an extreme level of attention to detail and professionalism by hand delivering the missing receipt, then I'll need to get a copy of this book over to Tree Trimmers!

Either way, I now have a new, preferred, landscaping company that

CHAIN REACTIONS

I would refer and recommend to anyone who asks - or reads this book. And that's what Chain Reactions is really all about.

So as you can see, whether your business is a bar, an auto dealership or even a landscaping company, The Red Napkin Treatment is just another practical, easy, and low cost method of creating the positive customer experience reactions that will keep customers coming back and have then telling others how friendly and good the service is at your business. Try it and you'll see the results.

Customer Experience Marketing

So just what is Customer Experience Marketing?

Customer Experience Marketing is the process of putting the customer experience first in the funding and execution of your overall marketing strategy.

Instead of just launching marketing programs focused on selling the features and benefits of your product or service, Customer Experience Marketing requires that you shift your focus and start asking "How do we create marketing programs that make customers want to engage with us? How can we educate customers better when they read or view our marketing materials? What is it truly like to do business with us?"

If you only do marketing to promote more product or service sales you're taking the commodity approach to doing business. Today customers demand more. Gone are the days of new product introduction email blasts and treating every customer like a number.

Today's customer expects personalized service. They want you to use the information they've agreed to give you in exchange for your promise to provide them with more value and an improved experience.

Additionally, Customer Experience Marketing is not the same thing as Customer Experience Management. It's not about "managing customers" but rather it's about focusing on improving the customer experience through engagement.

In fact, according to a research study conducted by Ernam Roman, customers equated the term Customer Experience Management with the perceived experience of "being manipulated." Something I'll talk about a bit more later.

So what are some of the key components of an effective Customer Experience Marketing program?

CHAIN REACTIONS

1. **Get buy-in from all your employees (if you any)**

    Because Customer Experience Marketing is a new way of thinking about your business and its marketing this new approach to growing your business can be hard for some employees to comprehend.

    Explain to them that marketing has changed. Tell them we now have access to incredible amounts of big data about our customers and that it's time we use the data we have to create better customer experiences on an personalized level.

    Tell them we have to rethink every element of our business processes and marketing plan with one strategic goal and purpose – to serve and create loyal, life long, customers.

    And never worry that you are over communicating this strategic goal and purpose to your employees. You can never say it too often.

2. **Segment your customers**

    Customer segmentation is the practice of dividing a customer base into groups of individuals that are similar in specific ways relevant to marketing, such as age, gender, interests and spending habits.

    In order to create the best experiences tailored to each individual segment you'll need to identify who your best customers are and then engage with each segment differently.

    Think about WHY customer are doing business with you and then send them special offers, educational content and personal follow-ups that are based on that segment's reason.

    Just remember that your business can't be all things to all people so pick your targeted segments carefully and then make sure your marketing speaks specifically to that segment.

3. **Make the experience effortless**

When it comes to the likelihood that a customer will do repeat business with your company, their past experiences relating to the "ease of doing business" becomes a critical factor in their decision to remain loyal or to look elsewhere.

Now like I mentioned earlier, Customer Experience is "in the eyes of the beholder" so the definition of "ease of doing business" will vary depending on the types of customers your business serves.

The key thing to remember is, regardless of the type of business you're in, B2C or B2B, the easy buying, delivery and after sales support experiences being delivered by companies such as Apple, Amazon.com, Zappos and other consumer product businesses are now the same "ease of doing business" experiences setting the standard for what individuals expect when they make a purchase on behalf of their B2B employers too.

Today, companies delivering B2B products and services need to realize that they also must provide their corporate customers the same levels of customer service and ease of doing business that they've come to expect in their personal consumer transactions.

In fact, the ultimate Customer Experience goal should be to make each and every interaction customers have with your business not just easy, but effortless!

For example, your Marketing must make it easy for current customers and prospects to find the online information they need (prices, availability, technical specs, etc.)

It must be easy for them to contact the people they need to contact (e.g. is your phone number on the front page of your website?) And most importantly, it has to be easy for them to make a purchase.

Make sure your product selection and checkout process is as simple and easy as possible. For example, if you're a B2B consultant or supplier, in addition to accepting Purchase Orders, consider offering payment plans, PayPal or credit card payments. Whatever it takes to eliminate transactional friction and make the purchase experience effortless.

4. **Look for experiential up-sell opportunities**

When it comes to marketing levers you can pull, there are three ways you can increase a businesses' revenue.

- New customer acquisition programs (expensive)
- Raise prices (not always possible)
- Sell more to existing customers (Up-selling)

Up-selling is where the most new revenue can be made and where you can see real benefits from Customer Experience Marketing.

For example, everyone wants to be treated special. It's just human nature. And if a customer can be treated special for "just a little more money," a portion of your customer base will be willing to pay that extra amount.

That's the reason for all the VIP specials and packages you see today; the premium level products and services available for just about anything.

To get the most out of your Customer Experience Marketing program, segment your customers by their willingness to pay and then tailor higher margin up-sell promotions and marketing around their specific wants.

CHAPTER 2

The Voice of the Customer

Let's go back to talking about perception versus reality for a moment.

There are two sides to every business: The inside reality of your businesses' products, people and processes (as experienced by you and your employees) and then there's the outside perception of your business as experienced by your customers.

What I mean by this is, it doesn't matter how many employees you have or how new (or old) the technologies you use to deliver your products and services are, the buying, delivery and support experiences your customers perceive they've had is all that matters.

As long as you can make your customers feel like they've had the most amazing, wow inspiring experience they've ever felt, they'll continue to come back for more of what you're selling.

And that's the beauty of differentiating on Customer Experience versus business size, technology, etc..

So what if your perception of the value your business delivers doesn't match what your customers are thinking and saying about your business? What should you do?

In a situation where your perception doesn't match the reality of how your brand is being perceived in the marketplace it's critical that you find out why. The way you can do that is by collecting and analyzing what is known as Voice of the Customer (Voc) feedback

Practical VoC Collection Methods

So how can you tell how emotionally connected your customers are to your brand, or how well their perceptions of your products or services match your perceptions?

This is where Voice of the Customer (VoC) feedback collection comes into play.

At the core of any Customer Experience Marketing program there must be an effective VoC feedback gathering process. In fact, VoC feedback collection is so important in today's business environment, analyst firms such as Saddletree, Ovum and Forrester, to name a few, have all identified VoC collection as a new megatrend in business.

And here's the good news: VoC collection doesn't have to be extremely complicated or expensive!

A practical VoC collection program balances its information needs versus the amount of time, money and effort required to collect the feedback using methods such as social media monitoring, online surveys, observational VoC and other VoC collection methods that engage both your customers and your employees.

When done correctly, and consistently, Customer Experience Marketing can convert the insights gathered from your VoC collection program into profitable business outcomes that can be tracked and measured using simple metrics and KPIs that we'll go over a bit later.

But before we move on, let me explain to you the very first step that needs to be taken before you start your VoC feedback collection.

Mapping The Customer Journey

The first step in any VoC feedback collection process is to identify and document the key areas, also called Touch-points, where customers most frequently engage and interact with your business. You can do this by creating what are called *Customer Journey Maps*.

A Customer Journey Map is a very simple idea: Basically it's a visual diagram that illustrates the steps your customers go through when doing business with your company.

Is it difficult to create a Customer Journey Map? That depends on the type of business you're in.

The more Touch-points you have with a customer during the buying, delivery and post sales service interactions, the more complicated (and necessary) a Customer Journey Map becomes.

For example, sometimes Customer Journey Maps take a "cradle to grave," look at the entire chain of the customer experience. Other times Customer Journey Maps can be used to look at very specific customer interactions; such as perhaps only focusing on the service department at an auto dealership.

A practical approach to Customer Journey Mapping would be to take a look at your business from a very high level perspective starting with the top five or six major functional areas (or processes) that cover the entire scope of your business and then discovering what are called critical "Moments of Truth" where a customer makes a decision to take the next step in the journey chain towards doing business with you or not.

For example, a Moment of Truth could be the point where an online customer decides to abandon their shopping cart because some aspect of their checkout experience is unsatisfactory.

Another example would be discovering that a high percentage of new car buyers are not bringing their car back to your auto dealership for service because some aspect of your service department doesn't meet their expectations.

These Moments of Truth are what differentiates the experiences and reactions customers have with your business from the all the other options they have.

So how do you discover where your Moments of Truth are?

Here are the top four things you'll want to look for and analyze when Customer Journey Mapping your business:

1. **Look for Key Actions:** What is the customer doing at each stage of their journey? What actions are they taking to move themselves on to the next link in the buying chain?

2. **Look for Motivations:** Why is the customer motivated to keep going on to the next stage in the process? What emotions are they feeling? Why do they care?

3. **Look for Questions:** What are the uncertainties, jargon, or other issues preventing the customer from moving on to the next stage in the process?

4. **Look for Barriers:** What structural, process, cost, implementation, or other barriers stand in the way of customers moving on to the next stage?

When looking for those Moments of Truth that are most relevant during a customer's journey, it can be helpful to look for those key Touch-points using some concepts first introduced by Google as well as those used by the Proctor & Gamble Company.

Those key Moments of Truth are defined as:

0. **The Zero Moment Of Truth (ZMOT):** By Google's definition "This is that moment when you grab your laptop, mobile phone or some other device and start learning about a product or service you're thinking about

trying or buying." It's that initial impulse when a potential customer decides to take action. It's when they see your ad in the paper or your website shows up in their search engine results.

1. **The First Moment of Truth (FMOT):** The next moment of truth to look for in your customer's journey is what Proctor and Gamble calls The First Moment of Truth. This moment captures what people think when they see your product or service offering for the first time, and the impressions they form when they read the words describing your offering. "It's in these first impression moments of truth that P&G believes you must focus all your efforts on converting shoppers into customers."

2. **The Second Moment of Truth (SMOT):** Also from P&G's thinking, is what people feel, think, see, hear, touch, smell and (sometimes) taste as they experience your product over some amount of time. It's also how your company supports them in their efforts throughout an on-going relationship.

3. **The Ultimate Moment of Truth (UMOT):** And lastly there's what Brian Solis coined "The Ultimate Moment of Truth." This is the moment when a customer decides to emotionally commit to their buying decision, or to advocate for your bran. It's that moment that creates the loyal customers we all want.

Customer Experience Marketing is all about making sure that each of these Moments of Truth and the chain of reactions they produce are presenting your business in the best possible light and that there are no Touch-points where customers give up on proceeding any further in the chain of interaction with your business.

If you look for these four key Moments of Truth when you design or review your businesses' Customer Journey Map, you can be sure you'll develop a Customer Experience Marketing program that leaves a positive and lasting impression on your customers.

Just remember, there's no single right way to create a Customer Journey Map. You'll need to find whatever format and level of detail that works best for your particular situation.

However, the concepts I just described should give you a good head-start at better understanding the Touch-points, journey steps and Moments of Truth your customers may travel as they engage with your brand, products, services and employees.

And that's the first step when creating your own practical VoC feedback collection program.

> 5%-20% -- The probability of selling to a **new prospect**
>
> 60%-70% --The probability of selling to an **existing customer**
>
> *Source: Marketing Metrics*

Non-Intrusive VoC Collection

Each and every day all of us, as consumers and as B2B customers, are bombarded with constant requests for our feedback.

Survey invitations fill in our inboxes. Our retail store and restaurant receipts ask us to "share our feedback" and automated callers on the phone ask us to "participate in a short consumer survey."

So the question is, how can you gather all the necessary VoC feedback required to improve those key Moments of Truth in your customer's journey? And how can you do it without annoying your customers to the point of producing a negative reaction towards your brand?

For example, how can you learn what your customer's biggest pain points are?

Or what other options they've already tried?

How can you learn who influences their buying decisions?

Or where they go to find answers and learn about possible solutions to their problems?

How can you go about getting the answers to these questions and more all without annoying your customers using online pop-up surveys, or dinner time tele-marketing phone calls, or any other intrusive contact methods?

The good news is, there are multiple other ways of collecting VoC feedback that won't annoy your customers.

Here are my top three, non-intrusive, VoC collection methods that many types of businesses should consider:

1. Observational VoC

2. Indirect VoC Feedback, and...
3. Software Analytics

Let's go over each of these methods in turn starting with Observational VoC.

Observational VoC Collection

A VoC collection method popular with many consumer product developers is to use what is known in academic circles as Ethnographic research.

In practical VoC feedback collection terms, we simply call it Observational VoC.

When using this method trained observers watch the behaviors of consumers as they go about their daily activities to see how they interact with their environments and to see how they solve their problems.

The key is to watch how your customers use your product or service at their usage location, or at any point in their Customer Journey where they interact with your business. For example, in a bank lobby, a dentist office or an auto dealership.

So how can you develop a good, practical, Observational VoC process?

A good process for conducting Observational VoC is the one described in "The Lean Six Sigma Pocket Toolbook" available at Amazon.com[3]

Let's go over the six best practices the Toolbook describes for performing good Observational VoC.

1. Be clear about the purpose of your observations. What role will the act of watching the customer play in the project? How will you use the information afterwards?

2. Decide when and how you will observe your customers (in

their workplace, in a retail situation, using online click path monitoring, etc, etc.)

3. Develop and test an Observational VoC data collection form for collecting the information you desire.

4. Always train your observers to make sure everyone will follow the same procedures and leave a good impression with customers who may or may not be aware they are being observed.

5. Always do a pilot with a few low-risk customers and tweak your methodology before rolling out your Observational VoC project in any big way.

6. For B2B companies, always include a follow-up with the customer if you've been observing them in their place of work. This can be done with a thank-you note, copies of your observations, updates on changes to your product or service made as a result of their contributions, etc.

Following these six best practices will keep you on track and assure you get the most value out of any Observational VoC collections you do.

Now before we move on to the next form of non-intrusive VoC collection there are a couple of downsides to using Observational VoC I need to point out; the biggest of which is that it can be expensive in terms of the time and money necessary to observe customers.

For example, if you're a window manufacturing company, having one of your marketing or customer service employees ride-along with one of your window installation crews can provide a tremendous amount of insight into your customers' unarticulated product needs and perhaps even your installation crew's needs.

But ride-a-longs can be quite expensive depending on how many you do and how far away they are from your home office. You'll need to evaluate the value of the information collected versus the expense required to obtain it.

Another downside to Observational VoC is that it can be influenced by what is known as the Hawthorne Effect.

The Hawthorne Effect is where the behavior of the subjects of a study are different due to their awareness of being observed – say for example if the window installation crew wears seat belts during your ride-along but don't when no one else is watching them.

I mention this just so you'll be aware of the Hawthorne Effect and are sure to consider its potential influence on any results you observe.

So with all that said, and even with these two potential disadvantages, Observational VoC can be one of the most practical, insightful, and best methods of non-intrusively collecting customer feedback for many types of businesses. Considering using it whenever you can.

On average, loyal customers are worth up to 10 times as much as their first purchase.

Source: White House Office of Consumer Affairs

Indirect VoC Feedback

Now let's talk about collecting indirect VoC feedback.

Indirect VoC feedback is any method that uses someone else to solicit feedback from your customers or someone else who experiences your Customer's Journey by testing your products and services as a proxy for your customer.

For example, many retailers and restaurants use mystery shoppers (or diners) as a way of getting VoC feedback related to how well (or poorly) their products, services or employees are performing.

Some other clever ways of soliciting indirect VoC feedback are pointed out by Chip Bell and John Patterson in their book Wired and Dangerous. [4] In it they describe how the mayor of Santa Clarita, California often meets with local hairdressers because they are likely to have the real story on what people have been saying about their satisfaction with the local government.

There's also the example of a hotel manager in Texas that schedules focus group meetings with local taxi drivers because he knows that his hotel guests are more likely to share their honest opinions with their taxi driver rather than with the front desk manager or in an online survey.

These are all good examples of indirect third party VoC feedback collection where the actual customer is not intruded upon and their need for remaining anonymous has less influence on their feedback.

Lastly, before we move on to our next non-intrusive VoC collection method, I want to point out one more example of indirect VoC collection that some may classify as Observational, but I prefer to classify it as just another form of indirect VoC.

Going Undercover

Have you ever seen the television show Undercover Boss?

This popular show features the experiences of senior executives working undercover in their own companies to investigate how their businesses really work, and to identify how their businesses can be improved to deliver better Customer Experiences.

In fact, Undercover Boss has become so popular around the world that local versions of the television show have been franchised in over a dozen different countries.

So why mention it here?

The type of indirect, undercover, VoC collection demonstrated in Undercover Boss can also be a good way for business owners and executives to non-intrusively watch how your employees interact with your customers during your customer's experiences with your business.

Go undercover yourself, or use a third party individual, and you may just be amazed at what you'll discover, for better or worse, about the things that are impacting your customer's experience and their reactions to your business.

So as a practical, time saving, learning tip, I highly recommend you look online for a past episode of Undercover Boss related to an industry similar to yours so you can see how this type of indirect, undercover, VoC could be useful in your business too.

Software Analytics and VoC Collection

Beyond Observational and Indirect VoC methods, businesses today have access to many software analytics tools and services that can examine the strength and pervasiveness of positive and negative social media sentiments on a variety of areas all without the need for directly engaging the actual end customer.

These types of non-intrusive VoC analytics can include:

- Speech Analytics for mining recurring word patterns in recorded telephone calls

- Text Analytics for analyzing text-based communications like email and postings on social media sites, such as Facebook and Twitter.

- Enterprise CRM Tool such as Siebel systems for capturing customer feedback as part of your Customer service or call center operations.

- and Mobile App solutions than can enable you to capture VoC feedback anywhere, anytime.

The important thing to remember is, don't use software tools (like pop-up surveys) that intrude on your customer's precious time and that could stop them from gathering more information about your business. Or possibly even keep them from taking the next step in the Customer Journey chain that leads to placing an order.

Make sure you use unobtrusive software tools that collect and analyze data generated by the normal engagements your customers have with your business.

And remember, no matter what business you're in, or the size of your marketing budget, today there are low cost, cloud-based analytics tools and services that can help you collect and process a wide variety of customer data into useful information that can improve your Customer Experience Marketing program efforts.

For more information on available analytics tools, you can check out the resources listed in the Resources section of this book.

> **80%** of companies say they deliver "superior" customer service but only **8%** of people surveyed think these same companies actually deliver "superior" customer service.
>
> Source: *"Customer Service Hell"* by Brad Tuttle, Time, 2011

High Tech Vs High Touch VoC Collection

Regardless of which VoC feedback collection method you choose, humans typically need to be involved. Essentially, you need to build a "people plus technology' VoC feedback collection process.

You'll also need to make sure that your people and tools are capturing the "right data." Meaning you'll want to collect information that helps drive sales or enhances your relationships with customers.

Just collecting Big Data for the sake of having more data will do little to move the needle on your customer loyalty and retention metrics.

So what types of VoC feedback collection technologies and analytics tools are available today that can save you time and effort without breaking the bank or requiring a PhD to understand their use?

Companies like Zoho.com and Batchbook.com offer affordable software analytics tools that are great for entrepreneurs and startups on a small budget. As a comparison, the annual cost for Salesforce.com is around $1600 whereas the cost for Zoho.com is around $300 per year.[5]

And these are just two examples of the new breed of "cloud based" software tools that are extremely cost effective and simple enough that any small business can use them.

However, it isn't always necessary to use the latest technology and tools to gather significant VoC feedback. This is where balancing your VoC information needs versus the time and effort required to obtain the information always needs to be considered.

For example, one Fortune 100 retailer that was heading into their peak selling season wanted to improve their website's user experience in an effort to increase their online sales.

Their problem was, their three month peak selling season was coming up shortly so they needed to act fast if they wanted to implement any new analytics tools and make any website improvements before their peak season arrived.

Now being a Fortune 100 retailer, this company could certainly afford to purchase just about any website analytics software or services they wanted.

So what high tech analytics tool do you think this big retailer selected?

None!

The best solution for their needs wasn't high tech at all!

Their best choice for implementing a quick VoC collection process was to use a low tech survey form that asked their Website visitors just three simple, open ended, questions.

1. What is the purpose of your visit to our website today?

2. Were you able to complete your task today?

3. If you weren't able to complete your task today, why not?

Pretty simple, right?

So why choose such a simple, low tech, survey approach over using Google analytics, heat maps and other high tech tools to analyze their Website?

The simple answer is, if you want to move really fast and you don't know anything about how your customers currently feel about your product or service, then it's usually better to just ask them what you can do to improve your offering rather than expending the time and effort to implement high technology analytics tools and then trying to figure out what's happening based on Website click paths and recurring text patterns.

Practically speaking, using a simple survey form with open ended questions, which are reviewed and acted on by human beings, will get you better insights into what your customers truly feel and want from your business much faster than you would expect.

So my key point here is, software analytics tools can be extremely useful and even necessary if you have thousands of customers and very large amounts of data to process. But for small and medium sized businesses, the fastest way to gain an understanding of your customer's feelings and problems can be to, simply, just ask them.

> Most employees only ask for the customer's name 21% of the time.
> *Source: ContactPoint Client Research*

REACTION CREATING TIP: Your customer has a name 100% of the time… And they like hearing it!

CHAIN REACTIONS

Do More Than Just Listen

So now that you've collected all this valuable customer feedback, how can you turn that feedback into profitable business outcomes?

Here's the hard, practical, truth: The real value of VoC feedback collection is not in gathering customer feedback, the real value is in putting that feedback to work.

You'll receive no Return on Investment (ROI) from just listening to, or analyzing, VoC feedback. You only get business results from actually acting on improving the customer's experience.

Effective Customer Experience Marketing must be a continuous cycle of activities that uses VoC feedback to Listen, Analyze and then Act on what customers think and feel about your products and services.

First, you listen to the feedback you're collecting via surveys, emails, customer calls, and comment cards.

Second, you analyze and learn from the review you do on that feedback so you understand what it all means.

And third you act on those learnings to fix the problem areas you've discovered based on the analysis you've done. You can't just stop with the listening part of the process.

So how can you make sure your business is taking the three necessary actions and achieving positive results from your Customer Experience Marketing program?

Well I'm sure it comes as no surprise that taking action on any VoC feedback collected is by far the hardest part of any Customer Experience Marketing program.

Here's why: In any Customer Experience Marketing program many of the improvement actions that need to be taken must be done by convincing other people connected to the business to take the necessary actions.

And getting people to take the necessary actions isn't always easy.

Many businesses have specific people in roles called Customer Experience Managers (CxM) that are responsible for the oversight and implementation of their Customer Experience Marketing programs. In online businesses, these roles are also sometimes referred to as Community Engagement Managers.

In most businesses, CxMs typically don't control all of the resources and processes that need to be improved and, therefore, can't implement the identified improvements all by themselves.

More often than not, CxMs only control the VoC feedback collection part of the process: which is why it's so tempting for them to just do more VoC feedback collection and not take any action on the feedback that's being collected.

To effectively implement a Customer Experience Marketing program, you (or your designated CxM) will need to influence and convince the other people connected to your business (your employees, external partners, and others) to take the actions required to improve the experiences your customers have when doing business with your company.

This ability to influence these other people takes a very special set of interpersonal and management skills that are really a mixture of part art and science combined with a balance of emotional intelligence and logic.

Now the good news is, these skills can be learned and used by business owners, or their designated CxM, to make sure a businesses' Customer Experience Marketing program constantly maintains its focus and momentum over the long term.

Because without someone in the CxM role championing your Customer Experience Marketing program on a daily basis, very little change is likely to occur that can positively impact the reactions your customers will have when dealing with your business. Nor is that change likely to be sustained over time.

Taking Action

So how can you, or your CxM, convince others to take the necessary actions needed to improve the Customer Experience?

One method I recommend is to simply maintain a prioritized "Top 10 List" of the biggest problem areas identified throughout your VoC feedback collection. Then every week have your CxM facilitate a meeting, or conference call, where this Top 10 List is reviewed by you and your Management Team to see what improvements have been made to those areas making the list.

Proving the old management adage that you "get what you inspect, not what you expect," this simple and practical process of reviewing a weekly list puts the continuous attention and priority on your Customer Experience Marketing program that's necessary to keep it moving over the long term.

You'll also find that the individuals responsible for those problem areas will be highly motivated to take the necessary actions to make the improvements that will get them off that highly visible Top 10 list.

Practically speaking, a Top 10 List is a simple and effective method of staying focused on the needs of the customer at all times.

So what other actions can be taken to assure a Customer Experience Marketing program remains on track?

Some companies employ much more elaborate methods of identifying the actions required to improve their Customer Experiences. However, elaborate and complex systems and technologies really aren't necessary in a practical Customer Experience Marketing program.

The reality is, businesses that are successful in applying VoC feedback to drive business improvements really just ask themselves two simple questions before developing and implementing their action plans.

Those two questions are:

1. Do we understand what the customer wants us to start doing, stop doing or to do differently?

2. What's our plan to make those changes?

Implement action plans that continuously address these two questions and you'll be well on your way to establishing a Customer Experience Marketing program that delivers real change that can drive significant improvements in your customer reactions, drive increased customer loyalty and ultimately deliver more profitable business outcomes.

Americans tell an average of 9 people about their good experiences, and 16 (nearly two times more) people about their poor experiences.

Source: American Express Survey, 2011

CHAIN REACTIONS

CHAPTER 3

Your Role As A Reaction Creator

*The meeting of two personalities
is like the contact of two chemical substances:
if there is any reaction, both are transformed.*

-Carl Jung

You sell just one thing: Reactions. The reactions you create are your product. According to Jon Taffer, star of Spike TV's popular reality show Bar Rescue, and creator of the term Reaction Management, *"Every failing business has an owner who first failed as an individual to achieve the right reactions in customers and employees."*

Essentially, if you're not achieving the business results you desire, it's because you're not producing the marketplace reactions you need to advance your business.

So what's the secret to creating the emotional reactions so necessary to build a lasting, profitable, business? There are five key areas:

1. All reactions are the result of the manipulation of people's emotions and how you can become a master manipulator (in a positive sense) to achieve the reactions you want.

2. Business owners who try to do everything themselves actually damage their brand and limit the potential growth of their business.

3. You need to more effectively manage today's rapidly changing technologies that are actually making our lives more difficult, not easier - and why those technologies that were supposed to make our lives easier have

actually put more work on our plates than one human can possibly handle.

4. You can actually save time and money while delivering better customer experiences by using an outsourced Customer Experience Manager (CxM) and why having an outsourced CxM that can handle many of your non-income generating activities is not a convenience, but rather, a necessity to acquire and keep customers happy in today's competitive Age of the Customer.

5. Learn how to hire and manage the right type of employees that will deliver the Customer Experience Chain Reactions you need.

So let's go over each area in more detail.

Manipulating Reactions

The word Manipulation gets a bad rap. It immediately conjures up the negative image of someone trying to take advantage of someone else in order to achieve personal gain. And that's too bad because Manipulation is just a tool that is neither good nor bad. It's really all how you use it.

According to the Merriam-Webster dictionary, the definition of Manipulation is "to manage or utilize skillfully." And let's face it, everything we do in sales and marketing is some form of manipulation to get customers to purchase our products and services.

So if you're going to be a success at creating Chain Reactions, you need to become a master manipulator who designs each and every link in your business process chain to achieve a specific, manipulated, reaction. And it all begins with you.

To paraphrase Taffer once more,

> *"You can't control everything that happens to you in business but you can control the reactions of other people and how you personally choose to do this affects your success. You are the first link in the chain of reactions your business creates and in large part your personal behavior defines how employees and customers respond to you and whatever you are selling. Say hello to a customer with a smile and you make a positive difference in their attitude toward what you're selling. Scowl at that same person or keep them waiting for twenty minutes and that will cause a reaction too. And it won't be pretty."*

Now if you don't like to think of yourself as a manipulator of people's reactions, another word for manipulation is persuasion and there are proven, scientific, principles that when followed can significantly increase your chances of influencing and persuading others. Let's go over a few of them now.

CHAIN REACTIONS

> "Although your customers won't love you if you give bad service, your competitors will."
>
> *Kate Zabriskie*

Getting to Yes – The Science of Persuasion

For years researchers have been studying the factors that persuade people to say yes. And it would be nice to think that most people make rational decisions based on informed, factual, information but the reality is 70% of all decisions are emotionally based while only 30% are rational in nature.

In the increasingly complex and "information overloaded" lives we lead today, people use decision "short cuts" to help them make choices. Researchers have found that these decision short cuts are based on six universal principles of persuasion that guide human behavior.

The six universal principles of persuasion are:

1. Reciprocity
2. Scarcity
3. Authority
4. Consistency
5. Liking
6. Consensus

Understanding these six principals (and how to use them to manipulate customer reactions in an ethical manner) can significantly increase the chances that someone will be persuaded to do whatever it is you ask of them. For example, getting them to enter their email address into a website form, shop in your retail store, buy more of something, etc.

Let's go over each one of these six principles in turn.

Reciprocity – This is the felt social obligation to give when you receive. For example, if a friend invites you to a party, then you'll feel an obligation to invite them to a future party. If someone does you a favor then you owe that person a favor in return. People are more likely to say yes to someone they feel they owe.

The key to using reciprocity as a persuasion tool is to be the first to give something and to give something personalized and unexpected.

Scarcity – This persuasion principle is based on the fact that people always want more of those things there will be less of. For example, tell someone that something will no longer be available after a certain date and demand for that item will typically go up. I'm sure you've experience this principle many times.

Authority – People follow the lead of credible, knowledgeable, experts. For example, physical therapists are able to persuade more their patients to comply with prescribed exercise programs if their medical diplomas are displayed on the wall of their waiting rooms. People are more like to act on a request from a person wearing a uniform than from a person wearing casual clothes. What the research has shown is that it's important to signal to others what makes you a credible, knowledgeable, authority before you make your influence attempt.

So when using the authority principle, the question becomes, how do you signal your authority status if you don't wear a uniform and you can't just go around telling everyone you meet just how totally brilliant you are?

The good news is, you can arrange for someone else to tell the world for you: think testimonials.

Surprisingly, research has shown that it doesn't seem to matter if that person is closely connected to you and is likely to prosper from the introduction themselves.

A great example of this is a group of real estate agents who were able to increase both the number of property appraisals and the number of subsequent contracts they wrote just by arranging for their reception staff to answer customer inquiries by first mentioning the agent's credentials and expertise.

For example, potential customers who called in asking about leasing a commercial property were told "let me connect you with Rachel who has over 20 years' experience in commercial real estate. I'll put you through now." Or if someone inquired about residential property they would say "let me connect you with Joe who has over 15 years of experience in that area."

The impact of these expert introductions led to a 20% rise in the number of appointments booked and a 15% increase in the number of signed contacts. Not bad results for a small customer experience process change that cost nothing to implement.

Consistency – People like to be consistent with the things they have previously said or done. Consistency is activated by looking for and asking for small initial commitments that can be easily made by the person you want to persuade. The key to using the consistency principle is to look for voluntary, active and public commitments and then get those commitments in writing if you can. For example, one study at a health care center found missed appointments were reduced by 18% simply by asking the patients (rather than the staff) to write down the details of their next appointment on their next appointment reminder card. A simple process change that is very effective.

Liking – People prefer to say yes to people they like. But what causes one person to like another? Research has shown that there are three important factors that determine who we like.

- We like people who are similar to us.

- We like people who pay us compliments.

- We like people who cooperate with us towards mutual goals.

Research has also shown that individuals (and groups) who exchange personal information and identify a similarity they shared in common prior to business negotiations were able to reach agreements 90% of the time as opposed to only 55% of the time when less personal negotiations were held. It is also interesting to note that the outcomes of the more personal negotiations were worth 18% more on average to both parties.

So the lesson learned here is, before you get down to business, make sure you look for areas of similarity you share in common with your customer and always give genuine compliments to them before you begin any engagements.

Consensus – When people are uncertain they will look to the actions and behaviors of others to determine their own. One hospitality industry study found that hotel guest staying for more the four nights were more likely to reuse their towels after small signs were put in the rooms stating that 75% of all guest staying in this room reuse their towels at least once. After the signs were put in place towel reuse went up 33%. So the lesson here is, rather than relying on our own persuasive influence, pointing to what others are doing: Especially many similar others.

So there you have it. Six principles of persuasion you can start using today to make practical, often no cost, changes in the way you engage your customers that can lead to big differences in your ability to influence and persuade them to take the actions you want them to.

We all need to begin thinking of ourselves as manipulators of positive reactions, deliberately creating chains of reactions due to our own personal behaviors. Done correctly and consistently, your customers (and employees) will both want to experience more of the same satisfying reactions and stick with you over the long-term becoming loyal advocates of you and your business.

But you can't do it alone.

The Lone Ranger Syndrome

Implementing an effective, business changing, Customer Experience Marketing program doesn't happen overnight and it doesn't happen all by itself.

It takes a considerable amount of time and attention to collect the necessary VoC feedback, analyze that feedback to learn from it, and then take the actions necessary to improve the reactions your customers have when engaging with your business.

And because you and your employees are already extremely busy people, it's imperative that you implement your Customer Experience Marketing program as efficiently as possible. That means having the right people doing the right things at the right time. Especially if you're the business owner or CEO where it's more important that you work on your business, by developing strategies and plans, rather than working in your business by answering customer support emails and other non-income generating activities.

Let's get practical here. Managing, or worse, micro-managing, every aspect of a business yourself is not only impractical, it's totally insane! Even the Lone Ranger had Tonto to help him get the job done.

No matter how you look at it, today's technologies that were supposed to make our lives easier have actually put more work on our plates than one human can possibly handle.

Office automation, Big Data analytics, video conferencing, all the technologies that were supposed to make our lives easier really haven't.

Technology has only made things move faster and requires us to continuously learn new competencies just to say even with the pace of business today.

As a result, today's business owners and their managers are working 12-14 hours per day and the personal sacrifices they are making are

CHAIN REACTIONS

huge!

They're sacrificing their health, their family lives, their personal relationships. All the things they say they're working for.

And it's all because they feel they have to do everything themselves; be on top of everything, every activity, every task. But it shouldn't, and it doesn't, have to be that way.

In real estate, there's a concept called "highest and best use" where properties are valued based on the best use of the land that will produce the highest value. In business, the same concept can be applied to people.

So let me ask you, are you and your people being used at your highest and best use?

For example, if you're a small business owner, where are you spending all your time? Are you doing things that could be more efficiently done by someone else?

Are you busy answering your own customer support emails, answering your own phone calls, making your own PowerPoint presentations, scheduling your own meetings, typing your own meeting notes?

And if so, are you acting quickly enough to assure your customers are happy with your response time and the quality of your responses?

It could be that your Do It Yourself attitude may be damaging your customer's experience and causing reactions you may not even be aware of!

As Michael Gerber points out in his seminal book, The E-Myth[6], you need to be "working on your business, not in your business." You need to be working on your business as a new product planner and a business strategist. Not in your business as just another employee.

I can't emphasize this to you enough if you're a business owner:

To deliver an exceptional Customer Experience, you need to move from being your own employee to being a true Entrepreneur.

You need to be working at your highest and best use where you have the time and freedom to enjoy your life while letting others work at their highest and best use to provide your customers the best possible Customer Experience.

Trying to do everything yourself just isn't a practical way to run a growing business.

CHAIN REACTIONS

Time Wasting Activities

As I said earlier, today's technologies that were supposed to make our lives easier have actually put more work on our plates than one human can possibly handle.

But what choice do you have? How will your business remain competitive if you're not up to speed and using the latest social media platforms, the latest online payment systems or the latest mobile App technology?

The solution lies in delegating your technology related systems and non-income generating tasks to other individuals so you don't need to be the expert in email auto responders, merchant account setups, Google analytics or social media monitoring tools.

The reality is, the way your business runs and performs (and the experiences and reactions your customers will have) are all really a direct reflection of how you manage your time.

If you're scattered, so is your business.

If you're disorganized, so is your business.

If you're running around like a `nut-case` trying to do it all yourself and controlling everything, guess what's happening to your business and the experiences your customers are having?

The reality is, if you want to create more satisfied and loyal customers, so you can achieve increased revenues, increased profits and increased free time for yourself, YOU HAVE TO STOP doing the low value things that take up all your time.

Things like:

- Answering your own phone calls

CHAIN REACTIONS

- Checking your email
- Editing your own videos
- Tinkering with your website
- Writing your own copy
- Writing articles
- Writing blog posts
- Doing the bookkeeping
- Installing Wordpress plug-ins
- Uploading files
- Playing with graphics
- Spending the majority of your time reading things on the computer.

Is this really working at your highest and best use?

Starting right now, today, you need to begin unloading and delegating every single one of these tasks to someone else if you want the kind of income, business and lifestyle you're imagining.

Every single task I mentioned above can be, should be, and MUST be done by someone else if you want your business to be known for exceptional Customer Experience Reactions.

So where can you find that special someone else? Your Tonto. That individual who can free you from doing these low value activities?

One solution is to outsource all these tasks to a talented, skilled, and trained Virtual Customer Experience Manager.

Outsourced CxMs

So what are Virtual Customer Experience Managers (Virtual CxM) and how can they help you avoid the Lone Ranger Syndrome that ultimately damages the Customer Experience in many small businesses?

Like many other Virtual Assistant roles, a Virtual CxM is an individual that can offload many of a businesses' Customer Experience Marketing program activities while also assuring that those activities are performed in a customer friendly and responsive time frame.

For example, some of the tasks typically performed by a Virtual CxM are:

- Responding to customer emails
- Returning customer phone calls
- Posting or updating answers to frequently asked questions on your website
- Responding to online review comments on websites such as Yelp or TripAdvisor
- Writing and analyzing online customer surveys
- Monitoring Social Media feedback
- Writing posts for blogs and social media channels
- Running and consolidating multiple analytics reports,
- Monitoring and reporting on metrics and KPIs

The list of tasks where a Virtual CxM can help you improve the Customer Experience is virtually limitless.

CHAIN REACTIONS

> 70% of buying experiences are based on how the customer <u>feels</u> they are being treated.
>
> *Source: McKinsey*

Finding a Virtual CxM

So now that we've covered what a Virtual CxM is, the next question is, where can you get one?

There are two typical methods of hiring a Virtual CxM.

Method #1 is to hire your Virtual CxM directly using one of the various freelancing Websites such as eLance.com, oDesk.com, Craigslist or some other similar online service where you post your job requirements online and freelance Virtual Assistants respond with their resumes and hourly rates.

The second way, Method #2, is to hire your virtual CxM using a full service outsourcing company such as Virtualhires.com or 123employee.com.

Full service outsourcing companies like 123employee.com provide pre-screened, trained and tested, "leased employees" that can provide a variety of services on a part time, full time or around the clock 24x7 basis.

You'll typically pay a bit more for your Virtual CxM if you use a full service outsourcing company (about $10 per hour versus $4 per hour) but the additional value the outsourcing company provides can free up even more of your time while assuring you get a reliable, high quality, Virtual CxM.

CHAIN REACTIONS

Using a Virtual CxM

The next step, after you decide where you're going to hire your outsourced Virtual CxM, is to determine how you're going use your new resource.

There are two common Virtual CxM strategies often used by small business owners depending on the type of business you're in and the types of customers you serve.

For example, some types of businesses lend themselves to having a Virtual CxM who interfaces with customers directly using email, social media or other communications channels, while other business types may be better served by having your Virtual CxM act as personal assistant to you or another employee who engages directly with your local customers.

Several businesses that are ideal candidates for using a Virtual CxM to handle customer service emails, perform online VoC collection, run sales analytics reports and other back office tasks would be online retailers, insurance agencies, software companies, product manufacturers, professional speakers, personal coaches and any other type of online information or product business.

Business that would be best served by using a virtual CxM as a personal assistant to a local individual would be real estate agents, dentists, doctors, landscaping companies, roofing companies, painters or any other type of local service where you or your employees require face to face engagement with the customer.

To learn more about where you can hire Virtual CxMs, and how to best utilize them in your business, you can find CxM task delegation worksheets, mind maps, interviewing guides and more in the resources area provided at www.ChainReactionsMarketing.com.

So remember, you don't have to do everything yourself. Getting a Virtual CxM is easier and less expensive that you probably imagined and having one for your business can be the game changer that will

CHAIN REACTIONS

put you ahead of your competition while also giving you a big part of your own personal life back.

Again, what could be better than that?

Happy Employees, Happy Customers

If your business has one or more employees then you need to recognize that their happiness with their job and their personal alignment with your business goals and objectives will, in large part, determine what your customers ultimately think and feel about your brand.

If your employees are happy and motivated, they'll pass this attitude on to your customers at all the critical Moments of Truth in the Customer Journey. If your employees are rude, argumentative or unresponsive when engaging with your customers, well I think you know how much that could influence whether or not you make a sale or retain a customer.

So the question is, what can you, the small business owner, do to hire the right employees and motivate them to deliver exceptional customer experiences that will keep everyone (including them) happy and loyal?

The answer is, the best thing you can do is learn from other businesses that are doing it right.

And when it comes to having engaged employees that are happy, trust worthy and loyal, no company is doing it better than online retailer Zappos -- which is why executives and managers from other companies like Southwest and Toyota often make regular pilgrimages to Zappos' Las Vegas headquarters to learn how the company achieves their incredibly loyal following.

Perhaps the biggest lesson I learned from studying Zappos' success is that their attention to hiring the right people that fit into their corporate culture is their "secret sauce."

Zappos's believes that the key to their success is having happy people working for them so they'll be successful in providing the best possible customer service - which is exactly what they do!

In fact, everyone who is hired at Zappos must go through a multi-week customer loyalty training course after which they are offered $2,000 to quit. By offering this "take the money and go work somewhere else bribe" Zappos quickly finds out if the new hire is truly committed and wants to be there, or not.

Zappos also believes in hiring lucky people. That's right. To maintain its unique culture, Zappos looks for specific qualities in its employees including weirdness, humor, humility, and, yes, even luck.

One of their interview questions is, "On a scale of one to ten, how lucky are you?" because (according to a study referenced by Zappos' CEO Tony Hsieh) people who reported themselves as being lucky are more likely to pick up on clues to help solve a task they were given. According to Hsieh, Zappos' goal is to "hire the lucky people that bring more good luck to Zappos."

In addition to hiring weird, humorous and lucky people, Zappos has developed ten core values which define their culture, brand, and business strategies.

They are:

- Deliver WOW Through Service.
- Embrace and Drive Change.
- Create Fun and A Little Weirdness.
- Be Adventurous, Creative, and Open-Minded.
- Pursue Growth and Learning.
- Build Open and Honest Relationships with Communication.
- Build a Positive Team and Family Spirit.
- Do More With Less.
- Be Passionate and Determined.
- Be Humble.

So the key lesson here is that it's the combination of corporate culture and enthusiastic employee dedication to delivering happiness through customer service that makes Zappos' stand apart from all other online retailers. At the end of the day you need happy, enthusiastic, employees to deliver happy, enthusiastic, customers and Zappos has cracked the code on how to do that.

CHAIN REACTIONS

> Customers are 75% more likely to purchase from a brand they follow on Twitter.
>
> *Source: Touch Agency*

Are You Their Boss or Parent?

So if the key to delivering exceptional customer experiences lies in hiring good people and placing them in an environment that encourages everyone to be themselves and use common sense to serve customers, then as I pointed out earlier "every failing business has an owner who first failed as an individual to achieve the right reactions in their customers and employees."

And one of the biggest personal failures small business owners often make is to keep underperforming employees because they "treat their employees like family." This is a major mistake.

Let's face it, most families are dysfunctional is some way or another and there's always one family member who would benefit greatly from a sever kick in the pants but never receives it because it's the nature of parents to be sympathetic and shield their weak and less capable children.

Now while it's true that you can't choose your family members, you can choose who you hire.

Profitable, well run business, rely on the strengths and talents of reliable and engaged employees who create energy and enthusiasm in everyone around them. Accepting a bad attitude and below expectations performance from any employee cannot be tolerated so you must never allow social or familial motivations make you accept a lousy employee that could cost you a customer. That's why it's important to always remember to "hire slow and fire fast."

CHAIN REACTIONS

Finding The Right People

As the business owner and founder of your corporate vision and culture, you can't afford to keep any employee who will "poison the well" when it comes to Customer Experience Marketing. Life is too short and business too competitive to tolerate and carry any individual on your team who is not up to the required standards.

Now I know you've probably heard this piece of advice before, but I'm going to repeat it here just to reinforce its importance to any businesses' ultimate success, and that is, the secret to hiring the right people (outsourced virtual employees or in-house local employees) is to hire people that have the right attitude.

As the old saying goes, "attitude is everything." And when it comes to finding employees who will deliver exceptional customer experiences, attitude is even more important than raw talent or previous industry experience. So how do you find the right employees?

Well as another other old management saying goes, always "hire for attitude, then train for skills." So let's talk about how you can "grow your own" Customer Experience Marketing superstars through employee training.

Note: To help you find the best employees I've provide a list of my favorite interview questions for Customer Experience Manager candidates in the resource section of this book as well as online at www.cxChainReactions.com/bookresources.html

CHAIN REACTIONS

Head Coach and Happiness Cheerleader

In wrapping up this chapter on "You as an a Reaction Creator" the last area we need to go over is your role as a coach, teacher and role model for your new Virtual CxM or internal employees.

In the Human Resource profession the word "training" is very common. Unfortunately, most customer facing employees won't really benefit from traditional training: Let me explain.

Training is behavior modification to react in certain ways to certain events. The problem with traditional training is that it takes too long and can't cover every possible situation a customer facing employee is likely to experience. In addition, traditional business training is often too structured to teach employees how to make the types of independent "common sense" decisions that are often necessary to deliver exceptional customer experiences.

What every business needs is employees that have been taught specific skills and then coached to use those skills to make their role in your business come alive. What they need from you is coaching.

Coaching is showing someone how to play a specific business role and then encouraging them to add their own personalities in order to allow them perform that role at their highest and best use -- after all, you just spent a lot of time to locate and hire the right personalities for your business so why would you then try to modify their behavior by asking these people to suppress the qualities that attracted you? What you want are employees who will use their unique personalities and talents to develop long-term relationships with your customers; not robots that have been trained to read a call center script.

It's really all about educating your employees in the areas that will make them better at delivering exceptional customer experiences and then coaching them to achieve the highest levels of individual performance they're capable of.

CHAIN REACTIONS

It's also about educating yourself about what it takes to run a high performance business that will attract and retain as many loyal customers as you want.

So where can you and your employees both get the education you need?

Two good resources for learning more about Customer Experience Marketing are www.Docstoc.com and www.Lynda.com.

And then of course there's my own www.cxChainReactions.com Website where you can learn more about my Chain Reactions Marketing System™ and practical Customer Experience Marketing principles.

In addition, business owners who complete my Chain Reactions Marketing System course will be eligible to join my Weisenberger Worldwide Success Network™ which is an elite mastermind group of like-minded business owners who want to grow and accelerate their business.

The Weisenberger Worldwide Success Network mastermind group provides business owners and solopreneurs with a network of experienced business mentors who are all experts in all aspects of business building who will help you take your business to a much higher level financially and personally.

By joining this elite mastermind group you'll benefit from the differing perspectives, input, and feedback you'll receive, plus the Weisenberger Worldwide Success Network can bring you resources and connections you might not have access to on your own.

If you're running a $500K+ business you'll benefit from joining this specialized group of like-minded individuals. For more information contact us at: www.cxChainReactions.com/bookwwsn.html.

So with that blatant commercial out of the way, (and a lesson to always be selling) let me end this section by saying, your role as the business owner needs to be that of a coach and cheerleader that encourages your employees to deliver exceptional customer experiences.

It's all a part of transforming yourself and your thinking from being your own employee to being a true entrepreneur who coaches a team and works on your business, not in your business, so you can get your personal life back plus make more money. And where have you heard that before?

If you do all the things we've covered so far in this book, how will you know if you're achieving a positive ROI for your time and efforts? That's what the next chapter is all about so let's move on.

CHAIN REACTIONS

CHAPTER 4

Reaction ROI

"A smile can cause a chain reaction of happiness"

-Eduardo Monroy

Now that we know what Customer Experience Marketing Chain Reactions are all about, what the benefits are and how you can delegate much of your Customer Experience Marketing program implementation to an outsourced, Virtual CxM, the next questions is: How can you tell if your business is actually making any progress and getting any ROI by improving the Customer Experience and its reactions?

How can you tell if your Customer Experience Marketing program is having a positive impact on customer loyalty numbers, creating advocacy or increasing your share of wallet with your existing customers?

In this Chapter we'll focus on a few simple and proven measurements that integrate VoC data analytics with customer life time value analysis to put the right financial picture into focus for your business.

We'll also use Practical examples of commonly accepted Customer Experience Marketing Key Performance Indicators (KPIs) so you'll learn how to look through the lens of your own business to see which metrics make the most sense for your business.

You'll also learn how to determine which customers are truly profitable and which ones are a drain on your time and energy, as well as how to measure and calculate the effectiveness of your Customer Experience Marketing program using field testing and customer feedback.

So let's get started.

CHAIN REACTIONS

> Always keep in mind the old retail adage: Customers remember the service a lot longer than they remember the price.
>
> *Lauren Freedman, President of The E-Tailing Group*

Calculating Lifetime Value & Profitability

Let's talk about the Return on Customer Relationships.

First let's look at Customer Lifetime Value (CLV) which looks forward towards the future and then about customer profitability (CP) that measures the past.

Unfortunately, CLV is one of the most overlooked and least understood metrics in business even though it's one of the easiest to figure out.

So why is this particular number so important to Customer Experience Marketing?

Mainly it's because CLV will give you an idea of how much repeat business you can expect from a particular customer, which in turn will help you decide how much you're willing to spend on your marketing and Customer Experience Marketing program to "buy" and keep that customer.

Now I could get all academic in the calculation of CLV, and talk about discounted cash flows and net present value, or tell you that you'll need to spend countless hours poring over spreadsheets and databases (or perhaps even pay thousands of dollars to outside consultants) but I won't because that's really not necessary for our Practical approach to calculating CLV.

For Practical Customer Experience Marketing programs, a Customer's Life Time Value (CLV) can be calculated using a very simple formula which is:

- The Average Value of a Sale times (x) the Number of Repeat Transactions times (x) the Average Retention Time in Months (or Years) for a typical customer.

An easy example would be the CLV of a gym member who spends $20 every month for 3 years.

The value of that gym customer would be: $20 x 12 months x 3 years = $720 in total revenue (or $240 per year)

Now you can probably see from this hypothetical example why many gyms offer free starter memberships to help drive new customers. In our previous example, the gym owner knows that as long as they spend less than $240 to acquire a new member, the customer will be a profitable member in a short amount of time.

Let's look at another example.

Have you ever wondered why there are so many Starbucks locations? Or why they have free Wi-Fi and comfortable couches?

It's because Starbuck's understands it's not trying to sell a $5.00 cup of coffee. Starbuck's is trying to acquire and keep a customer who, on average, will spends $24.30 per week, 52 weeks per year for over 20 years of expected customer loyalty. That equals $25,000[7] of expected Customer Lifetime Value.

That simple CLV calculation reveals a lot about how and why Starbucks approaches their marketing the way they do.

Now let's talk about customer profitability.

Are all customers created equal?

Most businesses recognize that some customers deliver higher margins than others. Typically, some of your customers will have higher costs to serve than others or they'll receive more benefits than others so that their net profit contribution to your business may vary.

It's with this customer profitability metric in mind that I need to give you a few words of caution about implementing a Customer Experience Marketing program.

Businesses that begin Customer Experience Marketing programs could become customer-obsessed rather than customer-focused. When the customer says jump they immediately ask "how high." Make sure you balance delivering exceptional Customer Experiences with the cost to achieve that exceptional experience for any specific customer.

So what are some other good reasons to measure customer profitability as a part of your Customer Experience Marketing program?

1. You'll validate that the actual service you're delivering matches your standard policy and business strategy.

2. You'll proactively identify any "leaks" in your profits and take the necessary corrective actions to improve things.

3. You'll be able to challenge the status quo of your current business structure to make sure that you maximize the value of your brand while also maximizing your profits.

Measuring Customer Lifetime Value and profitability is not an exact science. Cost allocations are not only difficult, but require internal alignment within a potentially large group of stakeholders who may or may not fully agree with the allocation process.

It's also possible that Customer Profitability analysis could reveal information that is not popular.

For example, what if you find out that one of your largest customers is not profitable and that service level agreement and pricing level changes will need to be made to what you currently provide them?

Or even worse, you may need to stop doing business with them all together!

It's only with the proper metrics in place that you'll be able to answer these questions and more about your Customer Experience Marketing program ROI.

Which leads us to our next topic.

CHAIN REACTIONS

Common Customer Experience Metrics and KPIs

As the renowned management consultant, Peter Drucker once said, "If you can't measure something, you can't manage it." And with that thought in mind, let's continue on with our focus on Customer Experience metrics and KPIs.

So how will you know if your Customer Experience Marketing program is making the financial impact you expected?

Here's some of the more common metrics used by businesses implementing Customer Experience Marketing programs.

Customer Acquisition Cost (a.k.a. CAC.)

You can calculate your CAC cost by dividing your sales and marketing costs (over a given period of time) by the total number of customers you picked up during that time period.

For example, if you gained 120 new customers over the course of a year and your total sales and marketing cost over the course of that same year were $1200 dollars, then your CAC would be $10 per new customer.

Now I know segmenting new customer sales and marketing cost from the sales and marketing costs required to retain existing customers can be an accounting challenge for some businesses but I'm sure you get the idea behind the CAC metric.

So how will you know if your Customer Experience program is giving you the CAC ROI you targeted?

Typically, you'll want to recover your CAC in less than 12 months otherwise your business will require too much upfront capital to grow.

You'll also want to see your average CLV number be at least three

(3) times higher than your CAC for any form of business with a recurring revenue model.

For example, businesses such as a membership Website, a fineness center, a landscaping service, or any other business receiving monthly payments would want CLV being three times their CAC.

Now let's talk about customer retention metrics.

Common Satisfaction Metrics

Customer retention metrics typically track measurements related to customer loyalty, customer advocacy and increases in customer share of wallet.

So let's talk about some specific and practical customer retention metrics we can track starting with a Customer Satisfaction metric.

C-SAT, short for Customer Satisfaction, is the average satisfaction score for a given Customer Experience.

You can measure C-SAT through a customer survey that asks customers to rate their satisfaction on a defined scale. Your survey would use adjectives that range from 'Not at all Satisfied' to 'Very Satisfied" or have them rate their satisfaction on a scale of 1 to 10.

Often the C-SAT metric is measured by customer interaction type.

For example, a product return, a password change, a simple question answered by email or some other Customer Experience that can be followed up with an automatically generated, post-interaction, survey.

C-SAT is just one of several customer satisfaction metrics that can give you an indication of how likely your customers are to remain loyal to your business.

Another good metric related to customer loyalty and retention is the Customer Effort Score (CES) which measures the relative effort required by customers to work through a given interaction with your business.

A CES is also measured on a defined scale using a post-interaction survey that asks customers questions such as: How easy was it for you to find the information you needed, place an order, make a return, or accomplish some other activity.

The CES metric can be a very powerful indicator that gives you significant VoC feedback related to the Ease of Doing Business factor I spoke about earlier. And remember, just because a customer says they are satisfied with your performance, that doesn't mean they will remain loyal to your business. Especially if it's hard for them to obtain the products or services they purchase from you.

So as a minimum you'll want to measure both your C-SAT Customer Satisfaction and CES Customer Effort Scores in order to get a clear picture of the customer experience reactions your customers are truly having with your business.

Customer Retention Metrics

When it comes to maximizing customer loyalty and the long-term CLV they will provide, the following metrics should be tracked by every business who has repeat customers.

Customer Churn Rate (CCR) which is the percentage of customers that don't make a repeat purchase or that cancel their service. You can calculate your CCR by taking the total number of lost or canceled customers divided by the total number of active customers over a given time period. This will tell you what percentage of your customers you are retaining over that period of time, usually measured on an annual basis.

Every business needs to know its CCR number and the direction its trending in order to understand how healthy your customer base truly is.

CHAIN REACTIONS

Lastly, no discussion of customer satisfaction and loyalty metrics would be complete without mentioning the often controversial, Net Promoter Score (NPS) metric.

The Net Promoter Score metric essentially measures the percentage of your customers that would recommend your business to their friends, family or colleagues by asking your customers the simple question "How likely are you to recommend us to a friend or colleague?"

Typically this single question is asked using a post-interaction survey using a 0-10 rating scale.

Your Net Promoter Score is calculated using the percentage of people giving your business a (9 or 10) rating (called Promoters or Advocates) minus the percentage of respondents giving your business a 0 to 6 rating (called Detractors.)

Respondents rating your business a 7 or 8 are considered neutral and are not included in this calculation.

Businesses considered world class expect to achieve a NPS of at least 50 while business receiving a NPS less that that would be considered just average in the area of customer loyalty.

Unfortunately, despite its popularity among many business executives, the Net Promoter Score concept has attracted some controversy from academic and market research experts who argue it isn't any better than other customer satisfaction metrics in determining the future loyalty of customers.

From a Practical Customer Experience Marketing perspective, the NPS score is easy to calculate and easy to understand so I recommend you evaluate it as one of the Key Performance Indicators your business tracks.

Regardless of what metrics you choose as the best fitting and most practical for your business, as I said earlier, "if you can't measure something, you can't manage it." and a Customer Experience

Marketing program is no exception to this rule.

Determining What to Track

For many business owners it can be difficult to keep from feeling overwhelmed by the sheer number of different metrics that could be used for measuring the Customer Experience Reactions. However, it doesn't have to be that way.

As is so often the case when analyzing anything, breaking down your Customer Experience Marketing program into smaller pieces and measuring only a few, high impact, high Return on Investment (ROI) areas first can make your tracking of Customer Experience metrics manageable.

When measuring the effectiveness of you Customer Experience Marketing program it's also important to remember that any metrics or Key Performance Indicator dashboards and reports you generate must be actionable too.

The users of your metrics and the recipients of your reports should be able to look at your analysis of the data and know exactly what to do about it. Make sure you provide context to explain what the data means.

For example, show how a metric compares with a target rather than just showing the metric itself because a NPS score of 60 means two totally different things if your target is 55 versus if your target is 90.

And remember, every business is different, but not so different that your metrics are totally unique. If you're struggling with how to take action based on your VoC data and Customer Experience metrics, know that you're not alone.

The good news is, there are systems, tools and people out there ready and willing to help you so you don't have to do it all yourself. One of them is my Chain Reactions Marketing System that we'll cover in the next chapter.

CHAIN REACTIONS

CHAPTER 5

The Chain Reactions Marketing System

When it comes to figuring out how to satisfy your customers so they'll remain loyal and refer you to others, do you feel like you're being pulled in a million different directions?

Are you somewhat confused about what you should be focusing on, right now, to win and retain new customers and are you unclear about how Customer Experience Marketing fits in with your other online and offline marketing strategies?

How about having a clear plan to follow that will show you how to win more loyal customers, more referrals and more on-going sales. Would you like that?

If you answered yes to any of the previous questions, let me tell you how the Chain Reactions Marketing System™ can bring it all together for you so you can build a booming business using Customer Experience Marketing.

With the Chain Reactions Marketing System you'll discover:

Clarity – You'll understand what customer's really value about your business and what it is that makes you special.

Consistency – You'll learn how to implement processes and systems to deliver the same awesome customer experiences over and over again.

Confidence – You'll become comfortable delegating non-income generating tasks to others so your business runs whether you're there in person or not.

Now if you're really serious about changing your business life and getting results, the way this training program functions is that you'll be given four, one-hour, lessons over a six week period and then you'll be encouraged to take specific action steps to implement what you've learned.

In fact each lesson will have specific actions steps listed at the end of the lesson, and remember, if you truly want to get the results, you must take action. You must implement the "home work" from each lesson or all the learning, all the time and money you invest, will be totally useless and totally wasted.

But, if you do follow through with the necessary actions, when you're done with the Chain Reactions Marketing program what you'll experience is a sense of clarity and direction, you'll know exactly where you're going with your brand and what it will take to create the Customer Experience Chain Reactions that will significantly increase your customer loyalty and lifetime profits.

You'll also have a sense of increased capability and consistency knowing exactly what skills, tools and assistance are required to implement processes and systems necessary to deliver the repeatable, awesome, customer experiences that will make your business and personal goals a reality.

Lastly, increasingly demanding customer needs change all of the time so it's important to have a flexible system in place to protect your business.

And because business owners are often too busy to satisfy customers who want more personalized service and attention from the people they do business with many business owners struggle to get results because they try to do everything themselves and don't delegate the low value, non-income generating, tasks that take up so much of their time.

With the Chain Reactions Marketing System I'll show you how to hone your Customer Experience Marketing delegation skills (and your unique strengths) so that you'll never have to worry about any unsatisfied customer leaving your business or posting negative reviews on social media sites or industry blogs.

In fact, when you finish my program I know you'll be a lot more confident that you can actually accomplish your business goals – even if you've been trying for years to build your business but haven't been as successful as you'd like to be.

So what's included in the program?

Let's go over the building blocks, the actual components of the Chain Reactions Marketing System.

In a nut shell, here's what you need to know:

- 6 week interactive course
- 100% Online
- Includes 4 training modules plus 2 weeks built in for implementation
- Each module includes training videos, cheat sheets, transcripts and all my presentation slides
- Plus weekly group coaching calls.
- No prerequisites to register (I'm going to turn you into a Chain Reactions Marketing Pro)

Essentially there are actually two parts to the program. The first part, four-weeks, is about systems and mindset where you'll learn about the importance of having an attention getting Customer Experience perception, the importance of creating personalized products and services when selling and delivering your offering and then, lastly, establishing a long term relationship with your customers that will deliver the lifetime profits that will keep your business running.

After that we will transition into the second, two-week, part of the program. Part two is all about taking action and putting together the pieces of the puzzle, the individual steps that it takes to build a local customer base or build a global online business.

CHAIN REACTIONS

I know that by implementing my Chain Reactions Marketing System you'll have the confidence to really move forward with rapid speed and clarity.

So if you're ready to join me and dozens of other forward thinking business owners who understand Customer Experience Marketing is simply the best strategy for moving their businesses forward, then check out my program using the following link and I'll give you a special bonus for reading this far.

www.cxChainReactions.com/bookbonus.html

> Getting service right is more than just a nice to do; it's a must do. American consumers are willing to spend more with companies that provide outstanding service ... ultimately, great service can drive sales and customer loyalty.
>
> *Jim Bush, Executive VP at American Express*

CHAPTER 6

How to Get Started

"Any good idea without action is just another idea in your head. Take action or you will never know the magnitude of what you could create!"

-Edward Squire

Congratulations! Now that you've been through this entire book I want you to know that I consider you a Chain Reactions "brother or sister in arms" so to speak.

The mere fact that you've put in the time and effort to read this entire book means that you're a forward thinking and committed professional that finishes what you've started. That discipline alone puts you way ahead of the crowd when it comes to having the vision and focus that's necessary to be successful in today's competitive business world.

So as one of my fellow authors, Jim Kukral, is fond of saying, "Doers get what they want, everyone else gets what they get." I couldn't agree more.

And because you're a Doer, who is ready to get started on your Customer Experience Marketing program right now, here's my quick and easy (relatively) four step plan that will get you off and running.

1. Take the Chain Reactions Customer Experience Assessment to determine where your business is on the Customer Experience Maturity Scale. You can download it here: www.CxChainReactions.com/assessment.html

2. Pick your Tonto. Decide who is going to be your Virtual CxM (in-house resource or outsourced.) Use the interview questions available at the link below to pick a Virtual CxM

who will be your sidekick as you develop and implement your Customer Experience Marketing program. www.cxChainReactions.com/interview.html

3. Register for the next available Chain Reactions Marketing System™ six-week training program. If possible, take advantage of the multi-student discount and sign up your Virtual CxM at the same time so you both can go through the training together. You can see when the next available class is offered here: www.CxChainReactions.com/bookcrms.html

4. **(Optional)** Sign up for the Weisenberger Worldwide Success Network™ (if eligible) which is an elite mastermind group of like-minded business owners who want to grow and accelerate their business. You can learn more about this exclusive program here: www.cxChainReactions.com/bookwwsn.html

Before we wrap up this section on getting started I'd like to point out, once again, that it's not necessary for you to implement your Customer Experience Marketing program all by yourself.

I'd highly encourage you to use the services of a low cost, outsourced, Virtual CxM to do the VoC feedback collection and analysis, as well as the publication of weekly KPI status reports.

I'd also encourage you to look at using an outsourced Virtual CxM to handle customer support emails, phone calls and any other time-sensitive customer interactions that would distract you from doing those highest and best use activities that only you can do – like closing sales and planning for the future.

If you'd like to learn more about how you can hire extremely reliable, yet low cost, resources from the Philippines, check out the link below and I'll tell you my story and how I do it.

www.cxChainReactions.com/outsource.html

CONCLUSION

*"It's not just thinking that changes our lives,
it takes action to make a difference."*

-Aaron Garrity

We're all in the business of selling reactions and the new Consumer Led Economy demands that the customer experience reactions we create must constantly meet the ever changing perceptions, preferences and buying behaviors of today's increasing demanding B2C and B2B customers. Business owners and managers who understand this shift in power will prosper while those who don't will be left behind.

So the question will always be, what do I need to do to delight customers and win their lifelong loyalty? And the answer will never be about price.

No loyal customer ever leaves a business because of price. They leave because of a lousy product or service experience and the lack of perceived value delivered.

So before I wrap up this conclusion, if I can impress upon you just one thought about beating your competition, it is: don't be cheaper, be better! Raise your customer experience level to match your prices; don't lower your price to match your competitors.

I also want to give you a brief recap of everything we just covered so you can begin developing your own Customer Experience Marketing program that I know will transform your business and your personal life.

First, I want you to remember that Customer Experience Marketing is a very simple and effective business strategy – remember the Red Napkin Treatment? Other businesses are using Customer Experience Marketing programs to grow their businesses and you can too.

CHAIN REACTIONS

Second, the best way to attract and retain more loyal and profitable customers is by providing customers a differentiated customer experience that generates powerful emotional reactions and stories they will remember and tell others. There's no one else in business exactly like you so make sure your customers come to realize that fact and choose only you.

Third, always, always, remember that your customer's perception of your business, and the emotional reactions they feel when doing business with you, is reality.

You must use constant and consistent VoC feedback collection to objectively measure and analyze what you need to do to provide your customers an exceptional and differentiated Customer Experience.

It doesn't matter how well you think you're doing, it only matters how well your customers feel you're doing.

Fourth, you need to understand that you can't do everything yourself and still deliver an exceptional Customer Experience.

You need to develop the confidence to delegate those time-wasting, non-income generating tasks to others so you can focus on doing those highest and best use activities that only you can do.

The best way to do that is to hire a Virtual CxM who can help you get your personal life back while also helping your business move the needle on delivering exceptional Customer Experiences.

And lastly, Measure, Learn and Act.

Focus on the three key customer loyalty metrics measuring Retention, Advocacy and Share of Wallet.

Find out which other metrics are the most practical and best fit for your business and make them visible everyday so they can drive behavioral change in yourself and your team. Do that and you'll begin to see your business results change in no time.

In closing, I hope the information in this book has shown you how creating great reactions from great customer experiences will earn your business the exceptional customer loyalty, advocacy and profits you so richly deserve.

I also hope you've learned that the key to long-term success, in any business, is to empower your employees and customers, respect them, and create a culture of genuine caring about them as individuals. Do these things and you will never lose.

CHAIN REACTIONS

Case Studies

Progressive Insurance

*Achieving Operational Excellence by
Putting the Customer First*

When it comes to making the customer experience as effortless as possible, few companies continually innovate as much as Progressive Insurance. Currently, Progressive is one of the largest auto insurance groups in the United States. Between 1996 and 2005, Progressive grew an average of 17 percent per year, from $3.4 billion to $14 billion.

Known for launching many industry firsts over the years, Progressive discovered long ago that making the process of obtaining and using auto insurance easy and less stressful would make them different in the industry.

As an example of their "make it easy" customer experience philosophy, in 1994 Progressive introduced the Immediate Response® Vehicle (IRV), a specially marked and outfitted vehicle that brought trained claims professionals to wherever customers needed them; even to the scene of an accident.

Using an IRV, Progressive's field adjusters show up at the accident scene, processes the claim and then write the customer a check - all right at the crash site. This makes Progressive's field adjusters more productive while delivering exceptional customer service.

Additional benefits of using IRVs include: first notice of loss is processed more quickly and cycle times are shorter which reduces their exposure to litigation. It also lowers Progressive's Loss Adjustment Expense by shortening the length of time its clients are forced to rent a car.

The key to Progressive's ability to fund this service is the cost savings it ultimately yields. Normally insurance providers are subject to fraud, with criminals making claims for accidents that were staged or never happened. Because of these and other types of disputed claims, Insurance companies also incur high legal fees – which, combined with the other costs of fraud, add up to some $15 out of every $100 in insurance premiums across the industry. Since deploying its IRVs, Progressive has seen costs in both categories plummet. Sending a company representative to the scene actually pays for itself while delivering a best-in-class claim processing customer experience.

In addition to its IRVs, in the early 2000s Progressive again changed its claims processes to focus on providing a better overall experience for every party involved in a claim, including the customer and the body shop. This focus helped Progressive launch a concierge level of claims service (another industry first) in 2003. With this level of service, Progressive oversees all elements of the claims/repair process on behalf of drivers involved in accidents, which reduces the time drivers spend managing repairs from about four days to 15 minutes. Customers simply drop off their cars at a claims service center and then pick it up once the repairs are complete. Progressive takes care of everything in between.

In 2006, Progressive expanded its concierge level of claims service to address the special needs of drivers whose vehicles not repairable as the result of an accident. Their Total Loss Concierge service helps customers find a replacement vehicle at a competitive price and helps them find financing, too.

Lastly, when it comes to acquiring new customers, Progressive discovered that providing an exceptionally easy quotation process that includes a comparison of competitors' prices (a convenience that many of their competitors have yet to match) actually lowers their costs.

For example, when providing quotes for a new customer policy, Progress provides comparison prices from other insurance providers along with its own. It's not that Progressive is determined to win the potential new customer by showing that they have the lowest price (in fact, Progressive has the lowest price quote only about half the time) it's that Progressive wants to look like they are an open and honest company who is looking out for the best interest of their customers by providing these competitive comparisons.

Providing this extra level of customer service during the Evaluation Link of the Customer Journey Chain accomplishes two things that actually deliver a positive ROI for Progressive.

First, providing this level of pre-sales service looks downright altruistic to the potential customer and elicits a trusting emotional reaction that may carry over into the next link of the Customer Journey Chain. Then, if the customer does eventually buy a policy, they will feel confident that they received a good deal and may even recommend Progressive to their friends and family: exactly the type of customer loyalty reaction Progressive wants.

Second, Progressive knows that its quote is the optimal price given the probability of that customer getting into an accident: a probability that Progressive is best-in-class at determining. If Progressive's quote is correct, then allowing a competitor to win that customer at a lower price is doubly effective because it frees Progressive from a money-losing proposition while burdening its competitor with the unprofitable account.

So as you can see, providing this level of pre-sales customer service and customer experience actually benefits Progressive even if they don't make the sale.

Overall, Progressive is delivering a level of customer experience unmatched in their industry which has led to phenomenal growth for them and their shareholders. Combine their exceptional customer service model with their quirky advertising and you create a differentiated Insurance company that attracts and retains highly loyal customers for life.

Zappos

Delivering Happiness With Happy People

Zappos is no longer just an online shoe store. Today they sell HAPPINESS: Happiness for their customers and for their employees. They do this because they've built a culture that is all about the customer experience and assuring that everything they do is focused on delivering more than expected.

For example, Zappos will take an order as late as midnight and deliver it to the customer's doorstep before breakfast the next day. If they don't have the shoe you want in stock in your size, they'll search competitors' Websites to try to help you locate what you're looking for.

Because of this exceptional focus on making their customers happy, 75% percent of Zappos business comes from loyal, repeat, customers despite the fact that their prices are almost never the lowest available online. Additionally, Zappos' loyal, repeat, customers ordered 2.5 times the amount that new customers ordered in the 12 months following a purchase, and had higher average orders. For example, in Q4 of 2007 first-time customers, on average, spent $123.86 while returning customers spent an average of $156.27 during that same period.

Because of their incredible success and customer loyalty executives and managers from other companies like Southwest and Toyota often make regular pilgrimages to Zappos headquarters to learn how the company achieves their loyal following.

A quick look around Zappos' headquarters reveals that a big part of their success is their innovative and quirky culture. Essentially Zappos' true competitive advantage is its culture. And no one inside the company is surprised.

In 2004, Zappos' biggest problem was customer service: specifically, finding the right employees to staff their call center. Today they have no trouble at all filling $13 per hour call center jobs at their Las Vegas headquarters.

Now a lot of people may think it's strange that an Internet company like Zappos would be so focused on telephone support when only about 5% of their sales happen by phone. However, what Zappos discovered was that, on average, their customers telephone them at least once at some point during the customer journey.

What Zappos also discovered is, if they handle the telephone call well they have the opportunity to create an emotional impact that will turn into a lasting memory and personal story that the customer will recall in the future as a positive customer experience.

With thousands of phone calls and e-mails coming in every day, Zappos views each and every one as an opportunity to build the Zappos brand into being about the very best customer experience. Their philosophy is that most of the money they might ordinarily have spent on advertising should be invested in the customer service experience so their customers will do their marketing for them through word of mouth referrals.

But perhaps the biggest take away anyone studying Zappos' secrets to success would come away with is their attention to hiring the right people that fit into their corporate culture. Zappos's believes that the key to their success is having happy people working for them so they'll be successful in providing the best possible customer service - which is exactly what they do!

In fact, everyone who is hired at Zappos must go through a four week customer loyalty training course after which they are offered $2,000 to quit. By offering this "take the money and go work somewhere else bribe" Zappos quickly finds out if the new hire is truly committed and wants to be there, or not.

Zappos also believe in hiring lucky people. That's right. To maintain its unique culture, Zappos looks for specific qualities in its employees including weirdness, humor, humility, and, yes, even luck.

CHAIN REACTIONS

In fact, one of their interview questions is, "On a scale of one to ten, how lucky are you?" because according to a study, people who reported themselves as being lucky were more likely to pick up on clues to help solve a task they were given. According to CEO Tony Hsieh, Zappos' goal is to "hire the lucky people that bring more good luck to Zappos."

Now if you think Zappos doesn't exercise any direction or discipline at all, consider their ten core values which define their culture, brand, and business strategies.

They are:

- Deliver WOW Through Service.

- Embrace and Drive Change.

- Create Fun and A Little Weirdness.

- Be Adventurous, Creative, and Open-Minded.

- Pursue Growth and Learning.

- Build Open and Honest Relationships with Communication.

- Build a Positive Team and Family Spirit.

- Do More With Less.

- Be Passionate and Determined.

- Be Humble.

So the key lesson here is that it's the combination of corporate culture and enthusiastic employee dedication to delivering happiness through customer service that makes Zappos' stand apart from all other online retailers

Mattel

Bad Move Barbie, Bad Move!

This next case study is a fascinating story about how Mattel (maker of the world famous Barbie doll) missed a tremendous marketing opportunity (and damaged their brand in the process) because they weren't listening to their Voice of the Community. What follows is an edited transcript taken from the Youtube video I did for this case study. If you'd like to watch the video version, you can see it here: http://www.youtube.com/user/JohnWeisenberger

Here's what happened:

In January of 2012 Rebecca Sypin and Jane Bingham got together and decided they were going to launch a Facebook campaign to see if they could get a bald version of Barbie made for young girls who had lost their hair due to cancer treatment. Their idea was to developed a "Beautiful and Bald Barbie – Let's see if we can get it made" Facebook fan page and see if they could gather enough social media community influence to convince Mattel into taking action on their request.

Within two or three weeks of putting their Facebook page online, the beautiful and bald Barbie Facebook fan page had over 100,000 fans as well as over 450 media outlets around the world that picked up their story and were reporting on how these two women were trying to get this bald version of Barbie made.

So let me ask you, what would you have done if you were Mattel? What would you have done if 100,000 Facebook users in your marketplace had a special request for your business?

Well let me tell you how Mattel responded. They did absolutely nothing!

Essentially they were silent throughout the whole first month of this growing Facebook community movement. And guess what happened?

CHAIN REACTIONS

Mattel's biggest competitor, MGA Entertainment, came forward and said they would be happy to make three bald "True Hope" dolls. Two girl dolls and one boy doll in each of its Bratz and Moxie Girlz product lines.

MGA also said they would donate $1-$2 dollars from the sale of each doll to help find a cure for childhood cancer.

So now about six weeks have gone by, and after their biggest competitor had said they would make bald versions of their dolls available, what do you think Mattel did?

Incredibly, once again Mattel showed absolutely no interest in listening to what was being requested by a growing number of their current and potential customers. In fact, one of their executives actually said that Mattel "doesn't accept ideas from outside sources."

So essentially Mattel told their Barbie fans, "No one tells us what to do"

So how do think that response was received by Barbie fans around the world?

Now flash forward some four months later, around April 2012, after an increasingly negative amount of global publicity was generated, Mattel finally decided to announce they would produce 10,000 bald "friend of Barbie" dolls but that they would only be available for distribution to hospitals and charities and this would be sometime later in 2013.

So let me ask you, how would you feel about Mattel right now if you were one of the Voices in their Customer Community?

For Mattel, this was actually quite a pivotal moment in their damage control strategy for dealing with all the backlash resulting from not immediately acknowledging the Voice of their Customer Community.

It's was also amazing that - still sticking to their "no outside ideas" message - a Mattel spokesman was quick to point out that Mattel did not create the bald friend of Barbie doll in response to the Facebook fan page, but rather because, "they helped us realize how important this was for us to do?"

Oh really Mattel...

So let me ask you, based on what you've heard today, what would you have done?

What if 100,000 Facebook users in your marketplace had a special request of your business?

Would know about it?

Do you know what is being said about your business, your brand, in your marketplace right now at this very moment?

Are your customers requesting any special or added features to your current products or services?

Are you willing to listen to your customers and react swiftly to their requests so you can spot new trends and jump on the next big thing? Especially when your customers say if you build it they will buy it?

The lesson we can all learn from Mattel's mistake here is that with social media it's imperative that you listen to your community. Be responsive and engage with them.

Mattel failed to do that. And when they finally did, they gave them a minimal effort plus they failed to give their community any credit for a really great idea; a very bad move on their part.

CHAIN REACTIONS

RESOURCES

Ten Really Useful Links

You may find these resources helpful when developing your CX program.

1. Youtube Video: The #1 Thing You Can Do To Increase Customer Lifetime Value: http://youtu.be/UwAKkyVlSA8

2. Worksheet: Six Easy Steps For Working With Virtual Employees: http://bit.ly/1lK5GpI

3. Handout: 5 Practical Tools for Online VoC Monitoring: http://bit.ly/1pm2sw7

4. Handout: VoC Survey Sample Questions: http://bit.ly/S35I44

5. HBR Article: Becoming Customer Experience Driven: http://bit.ly/1gZm61C

6. Zappos Slide Share Presentation: http://slidesha.re/1m6bsmQ

7. Article: Customer Respect, It's About Time: http://bit.ly/1plZSX5

8. Blog Post: On Customer Experience: http://bit.ly/1lK4Ysz

9. Businessweek Article: Customer Experience: http://buswk.co/1pm04Wl

10. Businessweek Article: The One Thing You Didn't Learn About Customer Service: http://buswk.co/1lK543k

CHAIN REACTIONS

25 Interesting Customer Service Statistics

94% of all online retailers provide email customer service.
27% of email inquiries are answered incorrectly.
Source: Zak Stambor, Internet Retailer, 2010

Almost 9 out of 10 U.S. consumers say they would pay more to ensure a superior customer experience.
Source: Customer Experience Impact Report by Harris Interactive/Rightnow,

In 2011, 86% of consumers quit doing business with a company because of a bad customer experience.
Source: Customer Experience Impact Report by Harris Interactive/RightNow

58% of Americans perform online research about the products and services that they are considering purchasing.
Source: Jim Jansen, Pew Research Center's Internet and American Life Project, 2010

Roughly 80% of customer service tweets are negative or critical in nature.
Source: Touch Agency

94% of all online retailers provide email customer service.
27% of email inquiries are answered incorrectly.
Source: Zak Stambor, Internet Retailer, 2010

24% of American adults have posted comments or reviews online about the product or services they buy.

CHAIN REACTIONS

*Source: Jim Jansen, Pew Research Center's
Internet and American Life Project, 2010*

81% of companies with strong capabilities and competencies
for delivering customer experience excellence
are outperforming their competition.
*Source: Peppers & Rogers Group,
Customer Experience Maturity Monitor, 2009*

The single most important thing is to make people happy.
If you are making people happy, as a side effect, they will be
happy to open up their wallets and pay you."
Derek Sivers, CD Baby

Smart businesses should come to realize that the customer
service bar is lower and that today, it's easier than ever to
differentiate your company from the pack with (crazy as it seems)
actual quality customer service."
*Brad Tuttle, "A Few Thoughts on the God-Awful
State of Customer Service," Time, 2010*

78% of consumers have bailed on a transaction or not made an
intended purchase because of a poor service experience.
Source: American Express Survey, 2011

In a 2010 E-tailing Group survey, only 10 of 100 online
merchants made the cut for stellar customer service.
*Source: Annual Mystery Shopping Study by
The E-Tailing Group, 2010*

41% of consumers expect an e-mail response within six hours.
Only 36% of retailers responded that quickly.
Source: Forrester Research Inc., 2008

24 hours or less is widely considered an
acceptable email response time.
*Source: "Email Customer Service in North American
Small and Medium Businesses" by BenchmarkPortal, 2005*

For every customer who bothers to complain,
26 other customers remain silent.
Source: White House Office of Consumer Affairs

It takes 12 positive experiences to make up for
one unresolved negative experience.
*Source: "Understanding Customers"
by Ruby Newell-Legner*

News of bad customer service reaches more than
twice as many ears as praise for a good service experience.
Source: White House Office of Consumer Affairs

It is 6-7 times more expensive to acquire a new
customer than it is to keep a current one.
Source: White House Office of Consumer Affairs

3 in 5 Americans (59%) would try a new brand
or company for a better service experience.
Source: American Express Survey, 2011

In 2011, 7 in 10 Americans said they were willing to
spend more with companies they believe provide
excellent customer service.
Source: American Express Survey, 2011

CHAIN REACTIONS

According to consumers, customer service agents
failed to answer their questions 50% of the time.
Source: Harris Interactive

80% of Americans agree that smaller companies place a greater
emphasis on customer service than large businesses.
Source: American Express Survey, 2011

In the last year, 67% of customers have hung up the phone
out of frustration they could not talk to a real person.
Source: Consumer Reports Survey, 2011

75% of customers believe it typically takes
too long to reach a live agent.
Source: Harris Interactive

12 Interview Questions for Virtual CxMs

1. Describe the most difficult situation in which you were directly responsible for overseeing the satisfactions of a customer?

2. What can be done in our business to help anticipate customer needs?

3. How can you make the relationship between yourself and your customer more personal?

4. Do you have difficulty admitting to making mistakes?

5. When was the last time you admitted to making a mistake?

6. When was the last time you made a mistake in servicing a customer, what happened, and how did you handle it?

7. Is the customer always right?

8. Give an example of a situation where a customer is not always right?

9. You are alone with a customer; your supervisor and co-workers are not around. The customer ask you a questions that you do not know the answer to. Answer correctly and they buy, answer wrong and they walk away. What do you do?

10. What is another term you could use for "I don't know" when dealing with customers?

11. What social media platforms are most useful in maintaining good customer relationships?

12. How have you dealt in the past with difficult or irritated customers? How did you handle it?

CHAIN REACTIONS

7 Practical Ways to Jumpstart Your Customer Experience Marketing Program

Ok, so you're convinced your business needs to prioritize Customer Experience Marketing and that as the leader of your business you need to stop doing the non-income generating tasks that keep you from delivering the exceptional Customer Experiences your customers want. Now you need to get started.

Here are some practical things you can do to jumpstart your Customer Experience program.

1. Take your office manager, operations manager or customer service manager (may be the same person in your business) to lunch to find out how they think the business is doing in delivering exceptional Customer Experiences. Ask them where they think the company is currently at and where they'd like to be, and ask how you can help. If Customer Experience Marketing Management is new to them share what you learned from this book to gain their interest. Then tell them of your intention to do some of the following steps. Note: If you plan on hiring a Virtual CxM, use this same type of conversation as part of the initial phone (Skype) interviewing process.

2. If your business has employees, set up a Customer Experience Working Group. Invite senior leaders and/or enthusiasts from each part of the business to participate. Alternatively, or in conjunction with the above, set up biweekly or monthly 'Lunch & Learn' sessions. Use these voluntary sessions to share ideas, delegate actions, showcase best practices, and educate across the company. If using an outsourced Virtual CxM, or other outsourced employees, use these recurring meetings to review ideas, review tracked metrics/KPIs and to provide any initial business or process training they may require to understand and support your business.

3. Create a Customer Journey Map by identifying every Touchpoint and Moments of Truth customers have with your

company and which departments are involved. There are dedicated agencies you can hire to do this for you or you could adapt this free Customer Journey Mapping Tool: www.cxChainReactions.com/jmtool.html

4. Perform a Customer Experience Maturity Assessment on you business to see where you are today. You can find a free template this here: www.cxChainReactions.com/assessment.html

5. In conjunction with your IT person or sales/data analyst (whoever collects your data) audit what customer data you have and how you currently leverage that information. Using your Customer Journey Map evaluate which tracking technologies you currently implement at every touchpoint where your customers interact with your business; Store, Website, Social Media, Support, Call Center, Direct Mail etc. Your overall aim will be to eliminate any gaps.

6. In conjunction with your data analyst and marketing person/agency, use data mining to build a marketing and sales strategy for acting on this data. Note: data mining is a task that should be outsourced to your Virtual CxM or other type of Virtual Assistant.

7. If you had any gaps, challenges, or problems undertaking steps 3-6, then you'll need to draft plans to acquire additional help to enable you to implement your Customer Experience Marketing program. There are many people and organizations out there that are ready and willing to help you. Don't be a "Lone Ranger" who tries to do everything yourself. Even the Lone Ranger had Tonto.

10 Tips for Writing Customer Service Emails

An effective customer service email response will keep your customer service costs down and help ensure the loyalty of your customers. Unfortunately, according to an Internet Retailer, 2010 study, 27% of email inquiries are answered incorrectly by customer service personnel.

To help make sure you don't fall into that 27%, the following are 10 tips on how to write a customer service email.

1. Address the customer's issue as quickly as possible.
    a. Customers expect their issues to be resolved in a timely manner.
    b. Wait no more than 1 business day to respond to the email.
2. Use an informative subject line.
    a. Include a brief description of the issue in the subject line. It should be enough to let the customer know exactly what the email is about without being too wordy. For example, if the customer emailed you with the title "Issue", it would be helpful to change the title to something such as "Instructions for downloading ABC software when using XYZ operating system."
3. Make the email personal.
    a. Address the customer by his or her name.
    b. Choose a salutation that matches the customer. For example, Andrew Smith, a medical doctor, should be called "Dr. Smith."
    c. If you do not know a customer's preferred salutation, then "Mr. Smith", "Mrs. Jones", or similar salutations should be used.

CHAIN REACTIONS

4. Use the appropriate tone.

    a. A customer email that contains insults or other aggressive language may cause you to become angry. Delay your response to such emails for a short amount of time to avoid lashing out at the customer.

    b. The first paragraph of the email should thank the customer for his or her email and provide a brief overview of the email. In other words, thank the customer and provide a brief answer, such as "Yes, ABC software is compatible with XYZ operating system."

5. Give concise instructions to your customer.

    a. This should be the main body of the email.

    b. Consider the customer's skill-level with regard to the subject matter.

    c. Provide easy-to-understand instructions that the average person can understand.

    d. Use numbers or bullet points to separate out each step that the customer must take in order to achieve the desired result.

6. Provide additional support information to the customer.

    a. Include a final paragraph that provides the customer with additional contact information if he or she has any other problems.

    b. Examples include that the customer should reply directly to your email with any additional concerns, contact a general email account, or a phone number to call.

    c. Provide a link for frequently-asked questions (FAQ) or a link to other useful tips to the customer.

    d. Let the customer know what times your customer support team is available for additional assistance.

e. Provide a tracking number, if available, for the customer to reference for future communications regarding the issue in question.
7. Close the email out.
   a. Thank the customer again for his or her email and for using your product or service.
   b. Provide your name. For example, end the email with "Sincerely, Joe Jones."
8. Proofread the email.
   a. Use a spell checking tool.
   b. Read the email and verify that there are no grammatical errors.
9. Send the email to the customer.
10. Don't Spam
    a. Do not use a customer's support request email to send offers or promotions after he or she contacts you for customer service. This may be viewed as spam by the customer and strain his or her business relationship with your company.

References

[1] HelpScout http://bit.ly/1m3rDA1

[2] Wikipedia.org http://bit.ly/1ryGSJC

[3] Six Sigma Toolbook http://amzn.to/1pJvi9S

[4] Wired and Dangerous http://amzn.to/RTIb5s

[5] Zoho vs Salesforce http://bit.ly/1pxoZJm

[6] The E-myth http://amzn.to/1ryIpQ6

[7] Kissmetrics http://bit.ly/U5FC23

About the Author

John Weisenberger CCP, is an author, speaker, certified business coach and founder of John Weisenberger Worldwide™, a premier global strategy and marketing firm that helps business owners and their managers achieve sustainable long term growth through Strategic Alliance and Customer Experience Marketing programs.

With over 30 years of Engineering, Marketing and Business Management experience, gained while working for large Fortune 500 companies such as United Parcel Service, Allen-Bradley Company, Rockwell Automation and Honeywell International, John has extensive knowledge of the best practices used by all functional areas of large global companies as well as a global perspective on the challenges of international sales and marketing and the nuances of managing strategic alliances and the customer experience across multiple cultural boundaries.

Today John is best known as the creator of the Chain Reactions Marketing System™ small business owners and entrepreneurs can use to expand their customer base, increase customer loyalty and drive higher profitability in virtually any market or industry.

If you'd like to learn more about John's background and offerings, just contact him at one of the links below:

Toll free: 1-800-473-2049, Ext. 301
Email: JW@JohnWeisenberger.com
Linkedin: www.linkedin.com/in/johnweisenberger
Facebook: www.facebook.com/John.Weisenberger.Worldwide

CHAIN REACTIONS

A Plea to Your Generous Nature

Before we finish I'd like to introduce you to a non-profit organization that is focused on helping small entrepreneurs around the world by arranging "microfinance" business loans for them. The organization is called Kiva and for as little as $25 you can help low-income individuals (who don't have access to traditional banking services) get their dream businesses off the ground.

As someone who is an advocate for global business and expansion of the world economy, I've helped finance several small businesses by making Kiva loans through my own business. As such, I'd like to highly encourage you to take a look at Kiva and see if being a "micro financier" may be right for you.

It gives me great satisfaction to know that I'm helping other individuals get their small businesses going and perhaps you might feel the same. To learn how I'm supporting Kiva, here's a link to my personal invitation page: www.Kiva.org/invitedby/john26356283

Thanks for your kind consideration of this worthy cause.

www.ingramcontent.com/pod-product-compliance
Lightning Source LLC
Chambersburg PA
CBHW030755180526
45163CB00003B/1039